FOCUS
the FAMILY
PARENTING

THE
LOW-PRESSURE
GUIDE
TO *Parenting*
········ YOUR ········
PRESCHOOLER

TIM SANFORD, M.A.

PRAISE FOR *THE LOW-PRESSURE GUIDE TO PARENTING YOUR PRESCHOOLER*

Twenty years ago, when I first became a mom of preschoolers, I was so overwhelmed with doing everything right. This left me rigid, tense, and overwhelmed. I wasn't having fun—and neither were my kids. Tim Sanford's message of low-pressure parenting is one I'm thankful for, especially since I still have preschoolers in my house through adoption! I highly recommend this book for parents who want to enjoy their kids and feel the weight of "rules" and "restrictions" slip from their shoulders. It's a book to read more than once and share!

TRICIA GOYER
Coauthor of *Lead Your Family like Jesus* and mother of ten children

Tim's book on simplifying the parenting process for preschoolers will change lives and help you to enjoy parenting! He compiles years of experience, knowledge, and wisdom from God's Word into solid advice urging parents to quit stressing about the mountains of input others provide them daily in order to raise the "perfect" child. He helps us transform our ideas of what we think we should be doing and instead form a plan for raising our children following God's inspired Word. I trust that God will use Tim's book to encourage many parents in the early years of their children's lives.

JOE WHITE
Award-winning author and President of Kanakuk Kamps

The Low-Pressure Guide to Parenting Your Preschooler by Tim Sanford provides a wealth of practical insight for the stressed-out preschool parent. I especially appreciated the "Big Four" low-pressure principles. Tim simplifies critical parenting tasks into an easy-to-understand strategy that left me repeatedly saying, "Yes! I can do that!" My two preschool grandsons and their parents lived with us for eight months this year, and I wish I'd had a copy of this book then. It would have helped me a lot in assisting their parents. Actually, it would have been easy to give them a copy of the book and say, "Don't stress—practice this stuff!" Tim's principles and insights could help a parent build a preschooler up and prepare the child for decision-making for the rest of his or her life. Thanks for this!

BRENT LINDQUIST, PHD
President, Link Care Center

Tim Sanford is a warm, encouraging, and practical voice for parents surrounded by conflicting advice and opinions for the "best" way to raise their children. You'll take a deep breath and smile with relief on so many pages—and you can replace worry with joy as you learn to celebrate and delight in the earliest years of your child's life!

CYNTHIA ULRICH TOBIAS
Author of *The Way They Learn* and *You Can't Make Me! (But I Can Be Persuaded)*

THE LOW-PRESSURE GUIDE
TO PARENTING
YOUR PRESCHOOLER

• • • • •

FOCUS ON THE FAMILY
PARENTING

THE
LOW-PRESSURE
GUIDE
TO *Parenting*
········ YOUR ········
PRESCHOOLER

TIM SANFORD, M.A.

TYNDALE HOUSE PUBLISHERS, INC.
CAROL STREAM, ILLINOIS

Editor: Liz Duckworth

Cover design by Beth Sparkman

Cover photograph of siblings copyright © nicolesy/iStockphoto. All rights reserved.

Cover photograph of boy coloring copyright © Tomsickova/Dollar Photo Club. All rights reserved.

Cover photograph of Asian boy copyright © hinata815/Dollar Photo Club. All rights reserved.

Library of Congress Cataloging-in-Publication Data for this title can be found at www.loc.gov.

ISBN 978-1-58997-867-6

Printed in the United States of America

22 21 20 19 18 17 16
7   6   5   4   3   2   1

CONTENTS

INTRODUCTION

"What's normal for my child to do at this age?"—*Amy*
"I have our son in soccer, piano, and a preschool
    reading assistance program. Is he getting enough
    socialization?"—*Maggie*
"How much (fill in the blank) is enough?
    Encouragement, downtime, sleeping, alone time:
    You name it, how much is enough?"—*Robert*
"Is age six too late to start our daughter in
    gymnastics?"—*Carmen*
"No matter what I try, I can't get my son to take a nap
    during the day. What do I do?"—*Heather*

These are comments from parents I know. Do they sound
familiar? All these parents have something in common and
probably something in common with you: They feel the
pressure of parenting correctly. As a parent, you're expected
to wear yourself out playing medic, professor, and chauffeur
to your kids—and make sure your kids turn out exactly right.
    There are books telling you what is exactly right, and

books detailing what to do at each stage of development to ensure your child *will* turn out to be healthy, happy, successful, popular, a good citizen—and a good Christian. Add to that the endless Internet articles to read and videos you "must" see to make sure you're doing just the right thing at the right time and just enough of it (but not too much of it), all to make sure your child develops properly.

I recently did a Google search on the phrase "how to parent," and about 590,000,000 sites showed up! Then I googled "how to raise children," and 385,000,000 sites appeared. I hope you're a speed-reader!

There's more, of course. Be sure to read all the magazines in your pediatrician's waiting area with articles such as "How to Be the Best Parent in Your Child's Preschool Class." And read every post on the *Mrs. Cleaver's Way to Be Perfect and Calm All the Time* blog.

While you're at it, remember the bazillion sermons, workshops, and small-group studies you should attend because the other "good Christian parents" are. With titles like "Raising Wonderful Kids in a Messed-Up World," "How Godly Parents Never Lose Their Temper," and "Christian Parenting the Right Way," you just have to attend and get all the information you can.

Once you've done all that, be sure to consider the whirlwind of contradictory advice from other parents and siblings, Bible study members, and the lady who scowls at you when your child has a fit in the supermarket candy aisle.

Finally, don't forget to compare your offspring against the other kids in the neighborhood, your church, and your

Mom's Morning Out group. Your child and your parenting are bound to come up short in at least half a dozen categories.

Taken all together, it's enough to make parenting confusing, if not crushing, with too much pressure, pressure, and more pressure. While having information is good when it comes to raising children, too much is still too much. It can confuse and discourage even the most dedicated parent, especially when there isn't enough time in the day to do it all correctly.

If you're like many parents I know, you're being stressed by many of these emotions and thoughts:

- self-doubt
- feelings of incompetence
- thinking you're a failure
- feeling out of control to the point where you either become paralyzed or run around the house doing a Chicken Little imitation ("The sky is falling!")
- wondering if your child is going to survive your parenting and turn out "normal"—whatever *that* is
- feeling you don't know the right things to do in the first place

You're feeling the pressure, aren't you?

Here's a dictionary-style definition of the word *pressure*:

pressure \ 'pres sure \ noun:
    A series of urgent claims or demands exerting a strong force on someone, causing a burdensome condition under which it is hard to hold up.

Demands. Strong force. Burdensome. Hard to hold up under.

Are we having fun yet?

It doesn't have to be that way. That's why I wrote this book.

I'm the dad of two daughters who are grown and married. I'm a licensed professional counselor with over twenty-five years' experience as a therapist working with children, teenagers, and parents. Before that, I was in youth work conducting church day camps, teaching Sunday school, helping out at vacation Bible school, and serving countless times as a camp counselor.

I'm married to Becky, who's been teaching elementary and middle school students for more than twenty years. So we've both been around kids awhile.

I don't claim to know everything, but I've learned a lot about what works—and what doesn't—when it comes to raising children. Through all that, I've discovered the key to understanding parent-child relationships—and making them more stress-free.

The key is coming to grips with *your true job description*: *what it is* and *what it isn't*. Seriously, that's the key.

The Big Four

Working toward that goal, I've boiled parenting down into four overarching, low-pressure principles to keep things organized in my mind and yours.

That's right, just four:

1. Shrink your job description.
2. Make friends with free will.
3. Step away from the power struggle.
4. Reduce the rules.

Apply these four principles and the rest is "gravy," as they say—good gravy, mind you, but gravy all the same.

Parenting is hard work, yet it doesn't have to be burdensome, leaving you feeling pressured all the time. You *can* relax. You *can* shrug off the pressure and know you're still parenting well. I want to help you understand your actual job description and accept what you can control as well as what you can't. Then we'll discuss how it applies to raising preschoolers.

"But what about the stress I'm under?" you ask. "What about all the pressure I feel every day?"

Chances are there's more *demanded* of you than there *is* of you. Where are you supposed to get enough energy or know-how to do it all?

Relax. Did God somehow make a mistake and create men and women with insufficient parenting abilities? How many generations of parents raised their offspring before the printing press was invented around 1440? How in the world did they manage without any of the materials we have today?

The problem isn't God's oversight, and it's not your lack of ability to carry the load of parenting. The burden, pressure, and accumulating weariness come from misunderstanding your job description. That's where the problem is.

What you're holding in your hands is not another "Do it this way and your child is guaranteed to turn out right" book. I'm here to explain to you your real job description as a parent—and how it's much simpler and less demanding than you probably think. My goal is to *shorten* your to-do list and relieve as much of the pressure as possible. I want to take the burden off your shoulders, not hand you another one. And give you permission to relax in the adventure called parenting.

"If I had it to do over again I would not spend so much time agonizing over every tiny detail of life I thought might impact my children in the long term, and just ENJOY their early childhood."
—*Shari (mother of two children, both teenagers now)*

Shari's a great friend of ours, and a great mom. Take her advice. Let's make this parenting privilege clear, simple, doable—and low-pressure. And by the time we're done, you'll be able to breathe a well-deserved sigh of relief—and ENJOY these early childhood years.

· · · · · · · · ·

SHRINK YOUR JOB DESCRIPTION

ONE

DO YOU HAVE TO MAKE THEM TURN OUT RIGHT?

CRAIG IS PART of the millennial generation, married and well educated. He wants to make a difference for Jesus Christ in the business world. Several years ago, he joined a small computer applications design firm comprised of five very talented individuals. But none of them—including the firm's founder—had any business management expertise.

Craig's frustration usually would come out in a loud, long sigh while we were cleaning our mountain bikes after a good ride. "I don't know what I'm supposed to do and what belongs to the other guys," he told me one day. "There are no job descriptions for any of us. We spend too much time checking things out with each other to make sure nobody is stepping on someone else's toes. We lose hours of work time that could be spent designing more applications! Our boss seems content to 'shoot from the hip.' I mean, that's okay if you want to stay small, but we have the potential to go really big."

Month after month Craig would hold out hope, asking for a job description. Month after month he was told, "Oh, we'll get to that. But for now, we have this really great job opportunity. As soon as I get them to sign the contract, we'll look into getting some job descriptions written up."

After about a year and a half of directionless frustration, Craig left the company. He and a coworker launched their own business. He told me, "The first thing I'm going to do is sit down and write out job descriptions!"

Ever have a job like Craig's, with no clear job description? It doesn't work, does it?

What's Your Job?

The business world uses job descriptions. So does the military. Even athletes have detailed job descriptions of what they're to do as part of the team.

Maybe you've composed a job description or two without realizing it. Perhaps you've given your babysitter one before going out to dinner with your spouse. It might look something like what Stacey, a mother of three, provides to her sitters:

"We have everything written out very clearly about our expectations:

• *Follow established bedtimes, plus or minus thirty minutes.*
• *Please have our children clean up any messes that they make.*

- *If the kids aren't getting along well, have them each do 'alone playtime' in their bedrooms for a specific amount of time.*
- *Please have them change into pajamas, brush teeth, read a story, and pray with them. A small light and music may be on.*
- *They are never allowed to watch TV—not an option.*

"Emergency information and phone numbers are listed as well. We always try to give a designated time we plan to be home by and then try to determine if the sitter is okay with that and whether he or she can be flexible. Seeing those specific instructions creates order and predictability in our home, and that's why I think sitters like watching our kids."

If business people, military, athletes, and even babysitters benefit from having job descriptions, doesn't it make sense for parents, too?

Yes, it does.

So where does the confusion and pressure of our endless to-do lists come from? You'll begin to see the answer if you ask ten people to describe the job of a dad or mom. You'll get fourteen different opinions. That's because the titles "Dad" and "Mom" have become vague, contradictory, and controversial. Often they're based solely on personal opinions or reactions to negative experiences. None of these things makes parenting more understandable or doable.

Since we tend to learn so much through contrasts, let me begin by addressing things that *don't* belong on your job description. Understanding what your job is *not* is as crucial as understanding what it *is*. It also helps relieve the pressure you may feel because of unrealistic or muddled expectations. We'll get to the *do* list in chapter 2.

Your First Impossible Mission

Naomi is the mom of a toddler who'd be classified as "all boy"—very kinesthetic, with the need to move and do.

"My son, Nathan, won't use words," she told me over the phone. "He prefers to communicate using sounds—machine sounds, animal sounds—you name it, any kind of sound. (Note: Communicating with sounds in place of words is a common trait for people whose primary learning style is kinesthetic, where learning takes place by carrying out physical activities.) We tested him, and he doesn't have any speech problems. How do I make him talk? I'm worried if he doesn't learn to stop using noises, he'll never get a girlfriend."

Did I mention that Nathan is only a toddler?

Behind Naomi's anxiety over a girlfriend is her desire to raise her only child "just right," so he'll grow up "just right" and find "just the right" girlfriend, who will become "just the right" wife for Nathan—all so Naomi will be happy having grandchildren to focus her time on, and all will be "just right."

Naomi doesn't have a dysfunctional child. She's a Christian mom who wants grandkids someday. She also wants to make sure her only child turns out right in order to be a good witness to her unbelieving family. Naomi was putting tons of pressure on herself and on Nathan as well—unnecessary and extremely burdensome demands.

Naomi's not alone. In fact, the single most common responsibility written into parental job descriptions is this:

"IT'S YOUR JOB TO MAKE SURE YOUR CHILD TURNS OUT RIGHT!"

Can you feel it? Pressure, pressure, *pressure*!

No, no, no. Even if that responsibility were accurate, everyone has his or her own interpretation of what "turning out right" looks like.

Do a reality check with me here. The first human home was the Garden of Eden. It was perfect. This perfect home was run by a perfect parent figure—God. In this perfect home with a perfect Parent were two perfectly created children—Adam and Eve. So far, so good.

In this perfect environment there was a rule: "You must not eat from the tree of the knowledge of good and evil, for when you eat of it you will surely die" (Genesis 2:17). That's as clear a rule as any parent can state.

You know the rest of the story. Adam and Eve chose to disobey God; they foolishly defied Him and ate the forbidden fruit. You and I live with the effects of that wrong choice to this day. We get old and die. Bad things happen all around us and to us. All of these things are sober reminders of that first wrong choice—made by a perfectly created person in a perfect world with a perfect Father.

So what did God do wrong? If He had brought Adam and Eve up "in the way [they] should go" (Proverbs 22:6), why didn't His children choose the right path? If it's the parent's job to make sure children "turn out right" (whatever that is) and God is the parent figure in this home, wasn't it His fault that His children did *not* "turn out right"?

If Proverbs 22:6 is a guarantee for all parents, why wasn't it a guarantee for the Author of the Book?

You aren't willing to say it was God's fault, are you?

You're exactly right, because it *wasn't* God's fault. And since it wasn't His fault as the parental figure, it's not *your* fault when your child makes an unwise choice, either. Let this settle in for a moment.

"But I *want* my child to turn out right," you say.

Of course. But that doesn't mean ensuring your child "turns out right" belongs on your job description.

"But—"

I hear you. That's your prayer, hope, desire as a parent. Yes, and you would do anything for your child. It's still *not* your *job*. Attempting to ensure that your child turns out right, or attaching your sense of competence as a parent to that goal, is where things go awry. It's *not* listed on an accurate job description for a mom or a dad.

So trash the notion that it's your job to make your preschooler turn out right. Doing so is the beginning of low-pressure parenting.

Your Second Impossible Mission

The second big responsibility that often sneaks into our job descriptions as parents is this:

"IT'S YOUR JOB TO MAKE SURE YOU DO
EVERYTHING RIGHT (PERFECTLY)."

Ooh. Even more pressure. Feel the stress?

You don't need to. God is perfect; you and I aren't. The good news is perfection is *not* on our job description. It's *not* required that you do everything correctly, know exactly what to do in every circumstance, or never make a mistake. That task is *not* on the *do* list.

"But I *want* to parent correctly!" you insist.

Great. But that's *not* part of your job description. God is not looking down from heaven with a clipboard in hand, evaluating your every move to see if you're perfect. Why? Because He already knows we're not perfect (and fully accepts us anyway).

Even if you are perfect in your parenting (as God was in the Garden of Eden), your child may still choose foolish things (as Adam and Eve did). On the other hand, you may struggle in your parenting through every stage of your child's development and he may still end up making wise, godly choices.

Que sera, sera.

In the Latin culture, where I spent my early years growing up as a missionary's kid, there was a philosophy regarding life and circumstances that was summed up in the phrase "*Que sera, sera*"—"What will be, will be." The deep influences of that culture help me see the truth in the following example.

As a concerned and competent parent with a young child's birthday party on the calendar:

1. You can be the best party planner on the block (doing it right).
2. You can put together the best birthday party a

three-year-old has ever been to (doing the right thing again).

3. You can purchase the highest-quality party favors and gifts, and the healthiest snacks money can buy (doing it right and having everything under control).

4. But if a snowstorm hits town, the power goes out, and everyone invited is homebound with two feet of snow piled in front of their garage doors, then your daughter's "best birthday party in the world" is canceled. Or the day before the big party, the birthday girl's older brother tests positive for strep throat and you have to disinvite everybody.

Que sera, sera.

You were wise and responsible. You did everything correctly. You controlled all the things that were yours to control. You are absolutely the best party planner on the block, no questions asked. Yet you still can't *make sure* the weather cooperates or your child stays free from strep throat—or that circumstances or children "turn out right." There is no guarantee, even though you did everything perfectly. It's *not* in your job description.

So scrap the notion that it's your job to do everything "right." Remember, we're talking about low-pressure parenting. Jesus was right in John 8:32 when He told us, "Then you will know the truth, and the truth will set you free." He was talking about His identity as God's Son, yet His statement is no less true for the rest of life. Knowing and understanding the truth—grasping reality—is what sets you free from the inaccurate expectations on your parental job description.

Our culture overemphasizes success—even in parenting. In an attempt to ensure your child will turn out right, you can be lured into grabbing control over the wrong things.

Most of us don't want to be control freaks, just "in control" enough to ensure our kids turn out to be responsible citizens and follow God with all their hearts. We think that if we control, we can make things turn out the way we want. We can be happy and avoid pain or displeasure.

Sounds good to me! you might think.

If only that were true.

You may not recognize it at first, because it seems like you can control your preschooler. Yes, it truly seems like you can—sometimes.

Remember When

Think about all the things you used to control when your child was an infant. You could schedule and regulate bedtime and bath time. You decided the type of food offered—though your baby ultimately decided what stayed in his mouth!

It's easy to think (a) you *can* control your child, and (b) controlling him actually *is* your job. With infants this works—mostly because they're too small to exert much active outright rebellion. Control-driven conflicts in parent-child relationships seem nonexistent—until your infant begins toddling. Then conflicts can become endless, and—if you follow a faulty job description—the pressure of parenting will really escalate.

But who has the final say about most of these life choices? Here's where things get confusing. As a parent you think,

Well, it's me, of course. I'm the parent and I'm the boss. The kicker, though, is that while you *are* the boss, ultimately it's your toddler who has the final say-so. Not so much with words, mind you, but with her behavior.

As she grows, so does her ability to exert her independence. Independence she uses to obey or disobey. Conflicts over the child's choice versus the parents' choice build and often become fully evident when age two arrives, if not before.

If you're like me, you're a concerned, loving parent desperate for your kids to turn out right, and you're willing to do whatever you can to make that happen.

Good for you. But you may be tricked into thinking the way to do that is by controlling your child. It's not. There's a huge difference between controlling your child's *environment* and attempting to control *her.* That's where this book comes in.

Your own expectations, the advice of others (expert or otherwise), and comparison with other families—all these factors put pressure on you and allow control issues to surface. The result—the kinds of struggles we'll be addressing realistically in the following pages.

A woman I'll call Jennifer would have benefited from understanding the concept of control. She had two daughters and one son, all about the same age as our two girls. As we got to know Jennifer, it became obvious that she was driven, talented, and success minded. It was also clear that she was determined to make sure her girls achieved great things. An elite swimmer in her youth, Jennifer never realized her dream of competing in the Olympics. She also got pregnant before her wedding and longed to redeem herself in the Christian community's eyes for her "one failure."

From the time her girls were preschoolers Jennifer pushed them, vowing that one was going to be the family Olympic swimmer (at any cost). The other was to be a sports physician for a professional sports team. That was just the way it was going to be. It didn't matter what either girl wanted.

"Besides," Jennifer told us, "they're too young and immature to know what's good for them."

The "future doctor" told my daughter, "I don't like it! Mommy doesn't even listen to what I want." This came from a *preschooler*. It's amazing how much kids pick up at a very young age.

As for her sister, the "future Olympian" turned all the pressure inward and had countless medical complications all through her childhood years. Doctors blamed stress, which Jennifer vehemently denied. Because of her *My girls have to turn out right* and *I have to do everything right* thinking, she wounded her daughters deeply their entire childhood.

Her girls are adults now. There is no Olympic swimmer in the family. There is no medical doctor, either. Mom didn't get either of the "successes" she pushed so relentlessly for. Last I heard, Jennifer's relationship with her now-adult daughters is strained at best.

Sad.

How You Think About Parenting

What do you assume a parent's job should be? Do you feel pressure to be the perfect parent or make sure your child "turns out right"? Do you feel the pressure not to parent the way you were parented?

To understand your assumptions, it helps to understand what you've been telling yourself. Your present thinking patterns grew out of your life experiences. And those experiences affected your thinking and decision making long before you ever thought of becoming a parent.

Your brain is complex. So to keep things simple, let's compare your brain to a jukebox. (I know, jukeboxes have been replaced by smart phones and streaming music, but today they're vintage and coming back into vogue.) An old-fashioned jukebox holds a wide variety of vinyl records, so imagine that each "record" in your brain's "jukebox" contains a brief phrase known as a *belief*.

belief \ bee 'leaf \ noun:
A statement of what you think is fact; a conclusion you hold about an object or circumstance you face—your perception.

You have beliefs about every subject under the sun. You use them every day to make sense of life. They're your "worldview"—all on a collection of records in your brain.

Most of your beliefs were recorded, cataloged, and stored in your jukebox during the first seven to ten years of your life. Here are a few examples of what I mean:

- "Boys are more important than girls."
- "Yellow is a stupid color for a truck, or anything for that matter."

- "All dogs bite."
- "No matter what I do, it won't be good enough."
- "Dogs make better pets than cats."
- "Anything below fifty degrees is too cold to be outside."
- "Crunchy peanut butter is better than smooth."
- "Do it right the first time or you're a failure."

Illusions in Our Thinking

Looking at your thinking is essential to your parenting. Errors, wrong thinking, skewed beliefs, and misconceptions lie at the root of many, if not most, conflicts. That's certainly true about parenting.

The formula for sanity is:
Truth, accuracy, reality = freedom, sanity, stress-free living (healthy thinking).

The formula for insanity is just the opposite:
Lies, inaccuracy, vagueness, errors = bondage, insanity, excessive stress (unhealthy thinking).

Here's where the pressures begin building long before you even know it. So this is a good place to start—thinking more accurately about this whole topic in order to undo common misconceptions about your role as a parent.

Regardless of how different your record collection may be from mine, we all have one that sounds pretty much the same. It says, *All my records, all my beliefs, are true. I can even verify them with real-life experiences if I have to.*

We're quite defensive about our collection too. Let's say I have the belief that "all dogs bite" in my mental jukebox. Is that record accurate?

"No, it's not."

But my defenses shout, *Do you think I'm stupid? I wouldn't believe a lie! I'm intelligent! I know what's right and true, and I can back it up with bite marks right here on my arm. See?* While I'm defensive with scars and all, my belief about dogs is still wrong and you're still correct.

When there are two parents in the picture (whether married, divorced, blended family, or whatever) there are *two* jukeboxes. This situation doubles the likelihood of error, wrong thinking, skewed beliefs, and misconceptions. It can also create a scenario where two different records are playing at the same time, both vying to be listened to—making for a not-so-harmonious-sounding environment. It also means there are *two* "But I'm right" records playing.

Be courageous and look at your thinking honestly. You may find some of your records are a bit warped and/or badly scratched. Some of your conclusions about what a parent is supposed to be or do may be based on incomplete information. Some of your records may need to be cleaned up, updated, or replaced altogether (like "All dogs bite"). This book will help you do that with records involving the subject of parenting.

When that happens, unnecessary pressures will come off your shoulders. Parenting may not become stress-free, but it will be clearer, doable, and more enjoyable. That's why the truth is so important, even in parenting—*especially* when it comes to parenting. The sooner you know the truth, the sooner you *and* your child will be free.

So shrink your job description. Toss these two moldy oldies from your jukebox:

It's your job to make sure your child turns out right.

It's your job to make sure you do everything perfectly.

Let's start over, creating your *real* job description as a parent. Helping you do that is *my* job description, as you'll see next.

TWO

RELAX: IT'S EASIER THAN YOU THINK

IF YOU CAN'T always trust your mental jukebox for an accurate job description for parenting, where does that leave you?

What are moms really supposed to do? And how about a list of assignments for dads?

I may be opening a can of worms by even mentioning gender at this point. Still, our secular and Christian cultures have traditionally assigned most parenting responsibilities to one sex or the other, things like who

- drives in the car pool every other day
- pays the bills
- leads the prayer at dinner
- cooks the meals

- does the laundry
- helps the kids with homework
- changes soiled diapers
- makes the older kids' school lunches
- drives the family on road trips
- mows the yard
- needs to be at the parent-teacher meeting no matter what

I could go on, but you get the idea.

In this chapter I explain job descriptions in terms of moms and dads, but that doesn't mean these descriptions are gender limited.

"Then these roles you're describing aren't etched in stone?" you might ask.

No, they aren't.

"Then they're negotiable?"

They can be.

"And they're interchangeable?"

Yes, they are.

"And if I'm a single parent, I can still do what needs to be done?"

Yes. It won't necessarily be easy, but you already knew that. Still, it can be done.

See, a *role* is the part someone has in a family, society, or group—or plays in a particular activity or situation. Parenting is the role you have in your child's life. Your role is not based on gender. It's not your identity. Your identity is who you *are*—the qualities, beliefs, and characteristics that make you different from others.

Gender comes into play when we look at the number one priority on a dad's and a mom's job description. While a dad can take on parts of either role, some of those tasks are more natural and easier for him because of the way God made males. That's all. Likewise, a mom may take on responsibilities from both roles; some are just easier and more natural for a female to do because of the unique aspects of God's image a woman reflects.

The job descriptions for a dad and a mom describe your role, not your gender or your identity.

I'm glad we could clear that up. Now let's close the lid on that can of worms and get right to what your job description really is.

A Dad Validates

A dad's primary, underlying job is to *validate* every one of his children.

validate \ 'val uh date \ verb:

To confirm, approve of, give official sanction to, or establish as legitimate.

Dads, in parenting terms, that validation means letting your preschooler know over and over and over, through words and actions:

- "Hey, you exist and you matter to me."
- "You're good enough!"

- "You belong in this family."
- "I love you."
- "You're an okay kid!"

Children get their earliest, most lasting impressions about who they are from what's reflected back to them by their parents. It's called the *looking-glass-self principle.* These impressions become those records that collect in the jukebox of your child's brain.

That was the case with Lisa. She was just shy of being three years old, petite, with blonde pigtails. One evening she waltzed into the living room where her dad, Brad, was reading the newspaper. Brad didn't respond. He didn't say, "Good to see you, princess." He didn't even say, "Don't bother me! Can't you see I'm trying to read?" Nothing.

Lisa began to doubt her own existence. As exaggerated as that may sound, it's true. It's that philosophical question: "If a tree falls in the forest, and there's nobody around to hear it, does it make a sound?"

The child's equivalent is, *If I walk into a room, and nobody notices or comments, do I really exist?* To Lisa the answer was *No.* Her existence was not *validated* by any response from her daddy. She interpreted that to mean, *I'm not important. I'm not an okay kid. I don't exist.*

Sure, that's the wrong interpretation. I know Brad, and he doesn't believe that for a second about his daughter. Brad genuinely loves Lisa. Still, that's how Lisa—and most children—will interpret this scenario. That's the way children's brains work.

"Not existing" is a scary proposition for young children.

So on that particular night Lisa marched over to where her daddy was engrossed in the paper and firmly sat down on his foot (he had one leg crossed over the other). Giving his calf a death grip with both arms, she pushed up with her toes and yelled, "Wheeee! 'ounce me, Daddy, 'ounce me!"

Later, when Brad shared this story with me, he sadly admitted he scolded Lisa for interrupting his reading time and shooed her off to find her mother.

Failure to do his job as a dad—verbally and behaviorally acknowledging Lisa's entrance into the room for a few short moments—led Brad to scold Lisa rather than validate her. That substitution doesn't work.

Notice, though, Lisa did get a response from her daddy—even though it was negative. By acting "badly," children can affirm they exist and that their existence has some sort of impact on the world around them. Their lives make "ripples in the water." At least Lisa got *something* from her dad, even if it was a scolding. It debunked the *You don't exist!* taunt in her mind, at least for that moment.

If Brad had just engaged Lisa with some light conversation, all would have been well, and he could have gone back to his newspaper. That's all it would have taken. That's it.

A dad's biggest job is to affirm that his child's existence—with or without any performance—is acceptable and good enough. If you're a father, recognize that your toddler or preschooler is worthy of being alive. You know that, but she needs to hear it, see it, and feel it from you again and again.

Value your child's personhood. Make sure your preschooler knows he or she *is* good enough for you. Otherwise, when that tree falls in the forest, the silence will be deafening.

Three Low-Pressure Ways to Validate

Since your primary job as a father is to *validate, validate,* and *validate* some more, that makes you the main validator. You're the one who affirms, *You belong here.* You give a sense of value when your actions say, *You're important, and worth responding to when you enter the room.*

"So how do you do that?"

Here are three simple ways.

1. Physically hold and play with your preschooler.

Healthy physical connectedness is critical during these early years. When my girls were toddlers, there were two activities they (we) absolutely loved and engaged in regularly. The first was "Bucking Bronco." You guessed it: I was the bronco, down on my hands and knees. Either taking turns or simultaneously, the girls would ride the horse around the living room floor only to be bucked off every so often. This would go on until my knees got sore. Then the bronco would fall over and go to sleep. It was lots and lots of healthy physical interaction, all in the name of playing.

The second activity took place outside. One at a time, I'd take my daughters by the hands and swing them around and around until we got dizzy. We'd gently fall down, and the two of us would roll in the grass, laughing. It gave me enough time to let the dizziness in my head clear before I would take my other daughter and do the same thing. Back and forth. Over and over again.

Don't expect Mom to do all the physical connecting. Your preschooler needs *your* physical touch too.

Try the same types of things with your preschooler. Toss him up in the air and catch him (safely, of course). Put him on your shoulders. Carry him on your back. Wrestle with him. If you have an especially physical, rowdy, kinesthetic son, be sure to "win" the wrestling match occasionally—not in a harsh way, but in a playful, safe way.

"Why? Won't that make him feel bad about himself?"

No, it won't. Your son needs to understand you're physically stronger and that you're the "alpha male" in the family. That means you're physically strong enough to keep him safe from life's boogie monsters. It also means you're physically the boss.

2. Keep your voice gentle and playful as much as you can.

Even though toddlers understand words, they understand inflection, volume, and tone better. Work to make your normal way of communicating lighthearted, upbeat, and pleasant. When correction is needed, see if you can turn the situation around by keeping that unthreatening tone of voice. Move to a lower tone, slower cadence, and sterner voice only when your lighthearted tone hasn't garnered the positive response needed. Even in correcting a negative behavior, you can do so in a non-attacking way and still get your point across.

"But, why bother?"

Understand this: *A child's mind is more open to hear and learn when your tone of voice is pleasant.* A lighthearted, upbeat tone means *I'm safe*; a gruff, staccato, or harsh tone sounds and feels like an attack—and translates to *Not safe! Not safe!*

Using an unpleasant tone will redirect your preschooler's attention to trying to get away from you rather than hearing what you have to say. Yes, there will be times when you need to use a louder, lower, slower, more powerful tone. That's to be expected. The rest of the time, however, keep your tone inviting—to help your child's ears and mind stay open to what he needs to learn from you.

By the way, use this same gentle tone of voice with your child's mother. It helps your toddler immensely, and it helps Mom a whole bunch too.

3. Keep your preschooler safe.

Let your young child venture into this new world, and be sure *he* knows you're watching out for his safety. You want him to know for sure that you will protect and rescue him if need be. And be sure you *are* there to rescue him if or when he needs it (as much as is possible, that is).

Like all toddlers, our daughter Heidi didn't have the life experience to distinguish normal pain from catastrophic "It's gonna kill me!" pain. I was assigned to take her to get her eighteen-month DTaP vaccination. When the time came for the injection, I held Heidi close to me. I began rubbing her back and whispering to her, "Daddy's right here. Relax, Heidi. The shot will hurt for a little bit, but it'll stop hurting soon. It's gonna be okay." Words, by the way, she couldn't comprehend—yet.

The poke of the needle came and so did the crying. The tears were her inner voice screaming, *Not safe! The sky is falling! I'm going to die! Help me! Rescue me!*

I kept holding her securely, kept rubbing her back, and increased the volume of my voice a bit: "Daddy's right here. It's okay, Heidi. The shot will hurt for a little bit, but it'll stop hurting soon. It's gonna be okay." Same words, same gentle and calm voice.

The nurse used the alcohol swab. The trauma was over—at least officially.

Heidi kept crying. I repeated, "Daddy's right here. Relax, Heidi. It'll stop hurting soon. Shhhhh. You're okay. I'm right here. You're okay. Shhhhh."

As I knew it would, the pain did subside. Heidi calmed down and gave me a little bear hug. The crying stopped. I wiped her tears and gave her a big bear hug, saying, "Good girl. You're so brave. You'll be okay. I know you will."

Finally, Heidi relaxed in my arms.

Validation brings a sense of safety, which is particularly important to preschoolers. It helps your child realize somebody is looking out for her.

That's *validation*.

"Really? *That's* the 'all-important' part of my job description as dad?"

Yes.

Relax and think, *validate*. That's your central goal. Ease the pressure on your weary dad shoulders, the ones you've worn out through overly high expectations and demands you—or others—wrote into your job description.

Is that all dads do? What about attending as many soccer games and dance recitals as you can, occasionally being the disciplinarian, fixing broken toys, and making sure that playhouse is solidly built? These things are important, and most of them validate your child too. Think of them as items on your job description; they're just further down the priority list. With the *validate* portion of your job description covered, the pressure of the endless to-do list is truly lightened.

A Mom Nurtures

What is a mom's primary job? It's not cooking dinner or checking Pull-Ups every hour. These are good things. Still, they're just "gravy" and they're lower on the priority list.

The most important thing on a mom's job description is to *nurture* her children.

> **nurture** \ 'ner chur \ verb:
> To nourish, support, encourage, train. To pour life into and help grow.

Moms, most of us have a vague notion about what nurturing looks like. Not being a mom, I asked some moms to help me out with a few specifics. Here's how they responded:

"Nurturing is filling your child up with aliveness."

"A nurturing mom takes the time to play, read, and take pictures when the child's Cheerios end up on his head instead of in his mouth. (We actually still have a photo just like this.) She enters the child's world to see things from his or her perspective, even if it means the carpets aren't vacuumed for a while. She provides empathetic understanding from a position of strength and support."

Before you feel burdened with a mile-long list you can

never complete—especially if you're a mom working outside the home—let me be quick to say that nurturing is not about "doing it all." And it's definitely not about doing it perfectly. It's about doing what you can without losing yourself or driving yourself crazy because your own needs aren't met. It's much harder to nurture your preschooler if you're exhausted. Remember, God didn't create you without the "enough-ness" to be a good parent. *The pressure comes from too many other demands placed upon you.*

You have permission to take care of yourself as well, as much as you're able. It may not be as much as you'd like. Still, do what you can. *You* need aliveness in order to pass it on to your kids. If you're a single parent, do what you're able to do; that's all you *can* do. In most cases, it will be enough. You'll find more ideas for single parents in the next chapter.

Three Low-Pressure Ways to Nurture

If the following tips sound like "Three Low-Pressure Ways to Validate," then you can see how the missions of dads and moms really *are* similar—but tend to be carried out in different ways.

1. Physically hold, touch, rock, and play with your child.

Your skin is smoother and softer than Dad's is. Your touch is gentler and your voice is naturally more calming. This is a woman's unique way of pouring life into her young child. When you play hide-and-seek with your child, you're infusing aliveness into that little person. When you scoop her up in a big, clean towel and dry her off after her bath, that touch is *nurturing*. I can't overstate the value of having a whole lot of physical connectedness with your preschooler or toddler. It's *nurture, nurture,* and more *nurture*.

If you have a child who's exceptionally wiggly or who doesn't like being held or hugged, that's okay. You can still provide the needed physical touch through play and through casual touch, such as when you show her how to hold a crayon or a spatula, or when you play "tackle" football with him. You also provide physical nurturing when you mend his cuts and scrapes.

2. Use a lighthearted tone of voice.

Your playful, gentle voice *nurtures* your child. It just does. And this lighthearted tone should not be taken lightly when it comes to learning. It's estimated that in a preschool classroom–type setting it takes around four hundred repetitions to make a new synaptic connection in your child's brain—that is, to learn something. In a playful/fun setting—like talking to your child at home—it takes as few as twelve repetitions to make that same connection. Where else will you get such enormous results from a simple, doable action?

"Just what's so different between my lighthearted tone of voice and my husband's tone of voice?"

Your voice more naturally imparts calm and an environment in which your child can learn all sorts of important things. In contrast, Dad's same lighthearted tone translates into a sense of safety and security and, therefore, your child's importance and belonging as part of the family "wolf pack." Moms and dads are just different, that's all; so are the effects of your voices.

3. Convey a sense of "You are safe" by attending to your preschooler's physical needs.

Keeping him safe can be as simple as helping him find his bedtime bear, fixing a cut on his arm, or making sure he has a snack when he comes charging in from playtime outside. All these little actions are declarations to your young child that you're making sure his needs are met, and that he's safe.

Your face smiling back at your little girl as you read her a story or rock her is telling her, "You're loved," and "You're being taken care of."

Stock up on colorful adhesive bandages (superheroes, princesses, puppies, etc.) and apply freely—even if the "owie" doesn't require one. That simple adhesive bandage is a visible reminder to your child that you've taken care of his needs and kept him safe.

"A silly Band-Aid does all that?"

Yes, it really does.

Another simple way you can send a nurturing "You are safe" message is to let your child wander. More than one mom has told me, "This is really hard to do!"

Not being a mom, I believe them. I'm not talking about wandering off to the other side of the mall or church grounds. To be clear, I'm not talking about wandering off in the middle of the grocery store or in a restaurant. Let your toddler or preschooler wander where it *is* safe.

"But if I let him wander off when we're playing in the open space at the park, he's going to want to wander off everywhere and all the time."

You're probably right. Still, you let him wander where

it *is* safe, teaching him which places are smart to wander in and which places are stupid to wander in. The smart list and stupid list will be discussed more in chapter 5.

"That's gonna be really hard to do because I have three kids who are all under five!"

Agreed. Still, do what you can when you can. And still let your preschoolers wander—maybe one at a time if need be. I'll state it one more time: We don't allow young children to wander whenever or wherever if it's legitimately not safe for them to do so.

When it's safe, let your child wander within your visual awareness. Start small—for both your sakes—and allow the wandering to develop slowly and safely. The preschool years are the time your child tends to venture off to explore the new world around her. Except when it's crucial that she stay by your side, let your daughter wander off and explore. Give her your verbal permission to wander—even if she didn't ask—which reinforces your position as the boss because *you* allowed her to go. Remind her you're right here for her, and acknowledge her when she comes back. This welcome-back thing is a big deal.

"Why?"

You represent her mobile "home base," her safe zone. When she circles back—even if you need to call her—praise her for coming back to you. Spend more time praising her return than scolding her for venturing off.

Besides, as you allow your preschooler to wander off—which she will naturally desire to do—it relieves some of the pressure you feel to keep him or her "on a tight leash" all the time.

You *can* relax a bit. Really.

Tell your child you're glad to see her—even if she's been gone only seven seconds. You're showing her you're happy she came back and that she's being cared for. *Nurture, nurture,* and more *nurture.* This venturing out and coming back is what builds your child's sense of safety; you're always there when she comes back around, and you like it when she comes back. It also encourages her sense of confidence. You're telling her, "You can do it!" That's why you let her go. Just be sure she actually sees you looking out for her. She needs that too.

Keep It Simple

Validate and *nurture.* Condensing your job description down to the "Big Two" is the beginning of lowering the pressure you feel as a parent.

If you let it, that is.

Unfortunately, many of us are so used to trying so hard that we can turn even the shortest job description into the longest ordeal. *Am I validating perfectly? Am I nurturing enough?*

If that sounds like you, help is on the way—in the next chapter.

THREE

HOW MUCH IS ENOUGH?

Dad, your *VALIDATION* doesn't have to be flawless. It doesn't have to be twenty-four seven, either. It just needs to be *enough* for your toddler. Mom, your *nurturing* doesn't have to be world-class or doing it all either. It needs to be *enough* for your toddler. That's it. Every child needs *validation* and *nurturing* to develop fully into a healthy adult, so you can be sure God hasn't made the task impossible.

"So how much is 'enough'? How do I know?"

Glad you asked.

Enough

The hard-to-measure concept of *enough* will make better sense if I use a word picture. Let's say you need fifty "units" of oxygen to stay alive. If you have fifty-two units, you have *enough* to live—maybe not enough to run a marathon, but *enough* to live.

If you have ninety-six units, you have *enough*—and plenty left over to run full throttle all day long.

But if you have only nine units, you don't have *enough*— and you die.

So if you have forty-nine units, do you have *enough*?

"No."

Exactly. But a parent might be tempted to say to a complaining child, "What are you bellyaching about? You have forty-nine units, and that's a whole lot more than the kid who only got nine!"

True, but it's still not *enough*—and you still die.

When I've asked clients if they got enough validation and nurturing while growing up, they've told me, "I know my parents loved me, and they gave me what little they could in the way of validation and nurture. I got more than a lot of other people did growing up."

I'm glad for that much.

But was it *enough*?

Some is not equal to *enough*.

The father of a girl who used to play with my daughters worked with college-aged singles. Her story still rings in my ears.

One day I overheard her say, "My daddy smiles when they (the college students) come (in the door), but he doesn't when I come in."

This little girl was part of an intact ministry family. There was no abuse or mistreatment, just *not enough validation* coming from her father. This simple unconscious gesture of not smiling when he saw her was interpreted as *I'm not important like they are.* The damage was as deep as if it had been caused by active abuse. In cases of *not enough,* the resulting pain, woundedness, and emptiness may be covered for years with a practiced smile, but it's still there.

Enough varies from child to child, personality to personality. What's enough for one child may not be for another. You find out how much each child needs as you study him or her. You do that by looking for answers to questions like these:

- What makes my child "tick"?
- How does he most easily take in my love?
- What makes her uncomfortable?
- Does she have to have a schedule, or can she flex?

As you study your child, you'll see what works for him and what doesn't.

When You're Parenting Alone

Single parents probably are more concerned—and knowledgeable—than others about the "How much is enough?" question. Their daily efforts to deal with this issue can teach other parents a thing or two.

These days, more and more households are single-parent families. Some don't technically qualify, but are headed by someone who's shouldering the parenting burden more or less alone. The reasons could be many:

- A spouse died.
- A couple divorced.
- A couple is separated.
- A parent has never married.
- A spouse has an addiction.
- A spouse suffers from mental illness.
- A spouse is active-duty military and currently deployed.
- A spouse travels extensively professionally and is gone much of the time.
- A single person adopted a child.
- Spouses aren't together because of legal, visa, green card, or passport complications.
- A spouse is incarcerated.
- A spouse is physically present in the home but is disconnected from parenting responsibilities and obligations.

Parents in these situations know how important it is to decide how much is enough. Most don't have the time or energy to do it all, even if they want to. In any of these situations, a parent has both the mom's and the dad's job descriptions to contend with. A single parent feels pressured to fulfill each description. I'll be frank: No one parent can do the job of two. It's not possible.

"So what *is* a single parent supposed to do?"

The answer isn't without its challenges. But largely, a single parent *can* still relieve the pressure he or she feels.

"But how? You just said I can't do both jobs."

Low-Pressure Parenting for Single Parents

Remember, the first of low-pressure parenting's four over-arching principles is to "shrink your job description." Since you can't do all the things a dad and a mom can do together, you must prioritize and place your energies where they'll have the best impact on your child. As a single parent, you will:

1. Physically hold and play with your preschooler.
2. Keep your voice gentle and playful as much as you can.
3. Keep your preschooler safe and care for his or her needs as best you can.

Does this list sound familiar? These three responsibilities for a single parent match those of both moms and dads. This is the same way dads and moms *validate* and *nurture*. These three tasks are the top three bullet points on a dad's job description and the same three listed on a mom's job description. And, single parent, you don't have six things to do—you have the same three duties on your job description. Do the same *three*—not six—things, and you're accomplishing your job description as a single parent.

A single parent *can validate* and *nurture enough* and raise a healthy human being. Make these two responsibilities—*validate* and *nurture*—your central focus. Accept the fact that all the other things that need to be done—or that other people expect you to do—are secondary. With these runner-up tasks, you choose which ones will be done and which ones won't.

While I was in graduate school, we lived in a town house

complex called Queen Anne Way. I was working retail full-time as well as going to school full-time. Becky was a stay-at-home mom with our daughters and brought in needed additional income by being the full-time caretaker of a four-and-a-half-year-old little guy named Tommy.

Tommy's mom, Elena, was a single mother, and like most single parents, she had to work full-time in order to pay the bills. One evening as Elena was picking Tommy up, she shared with Becky: "I wandered away from God and my church family after I graduated from high school. I met a guy and we fell in love—at least I fell in love with him. I got pregnant, only to find out he had no intention of staying around. I was all alone."

Elena later made amends with her parents and her church family. She also accepted her situation in life as a single parent and adored Tommy. She doted on him, disciplined him, played with him, and signed him up for activities at church that were led by men who could serve as healthy role models.

Elena was being a great parent.

Was she doing it *all*?

No.

Was she *trying* to do it all?

No.

She wasn't fighting the realities of her situation. She was *validating* and *nurturing* Tommy.

Yes, it was hard. Elena admitted that openly and often to Becky. And yes, it was worth it. She was parenting well as a single mom.

Parents who *aren't* single can learn from Elena's example. Every parent has limited energy and emotional resources.

With two healthy parents in the home, each can relax a bit on allocating those resources. But when you're the only parent in the home, managing those limited resources becomes a necessity.

So do what you can, not what you can't. And realize it's okay: *Your child can still turn out fine and be well adjusted.*

If you're a single parent, to cover the "dad" part of parenting, remember to *validate*. To cover the "mom" part, *nurture*. Mission accomplished on both fronts.

Yes, some of the "gravy" things will go undone. That's okay. You're not a failure. Cover *validate* and *nurture*—which can be done by a single parent—and give yourself grace for the things that don't get done. Take the pressure to "do it all" off your shoulders and heart.

Pulling double shifts as a single parent is tiring and difficult. Consolidating the two job descriptions into a *doable* one lowers the pressure. You don't have to do it all, and no one should expect you to.

All-important does not equal *complicated*.

Keep it simple.

Hold, hug, romp, wrestle, cuddle, and carry your preschooler around.

Talk, sing, read, whisper, and laugh with her.

Keep him physically safe, caring for his needs as best you can.

Redefine Success

Regardless of your parenting situation, you can erase *make sure they turn out right* and *make sure you do everything exactly right* from your job description. Add *validate* and *nurture* and you'll be a successful parent.

All that fine print about paying for things, coaching your daughter's soccer team, correcting your son's awful table manners, sitting through countless piano recitals, teaching spiritual values, driving all over town, disciplining, encouraging, saying no at times and yes at other times, setting boundaries, and repeating all this as needed are items on your job description too. They're just further down on the priority list. This is the "gravy" stuff. Good gravy, remember, but still gravy.

Get into the mind-set that everything you do as a parent ultimately is part of *validating* or *nurturing* your young child. Don't forget it's not about being perfect or "doing it all."

It's about "enough."

Relax. You *can* do these things. And while there may be hard times, you can manage the pressure *successfully.* Remember, the results aren't in your hands. The clearer you are about your job description, the more you can maintain a balanced approach to this thing called parenting.

Ask for Feedback

If you're not sure whether your approach to parenting is *enough*, get some feedback. Ask your spouse or a close friend or an older parent—someone you trust and who knows you well. You might even talk with the children's pastor at your church or some of the older, wiser children's Sunday school teachers. There's no need to guess and hope. Ask—it's okay!

What else can you do to ensure that your "enough" is really enough?

You can pray.

That may sound like an overly obvious statement to make in a Christian book on parenting, but I'll say it anyway. Ask God to show you how to be a healthy parent to your child. Ask Him to be your preschooler's Protector—physically, emotionally, and spiritually.

The simple act of praying for your child does several important things for you, too:

- It tends to keep you humble.
- It reminds you that you really don't know it all and that you need God's help every day.
- It slows your thinking down for a few minutes and allows you time to reflect.

For moms, it's a huge act of *nurturing*—even if your child doesn't know you're doing it. You're caring for his needs by praying about them.

For dads, it's a huge act of *validating*—again, even if your child doesn't know. You're verbalizing to God and yourself that she exists, that she's worth praying for, and that she's worth the investment of learning how to parent her even more effectively.

So pray. This is far more valuable than I realized when I was a young dad. Looking back I can see it now, but back then it just sounded like another nice Christian saying. Believe me, it's not. It's *huge* for you and that toddler or preschooler of yours.

No matter what your situation, stick to your real job description, and you'll find it's enough.

By the way, all the brain development that goes on during these busy preschool years? You're providing for that when you *validate* and *nurture*. And the developmental stages your child is growing through? You're helping him navigate successfully.

Remember, validating means letting your toddler know these truths repeatedly, through words and actions:

- "Hey, you exist and you matter to me."
- "You're good enough!"
- "You belong in this family."
- "You're an okay kid!"

Nurturing means to nourish, support, and encourage. It means to pour aliveness into your young child, and it helps him or her grow.

Validate. Nurture. And relax.

All the rest—yes, *all* the rest—is "gravy."

FOUR

AVOID THESE STRESS TRAPS

YOUR JOB DESCRIPTION *IS* DOABLE.

You *can* validate.

You *can* nurture.

And it *can* be enough.

That's not to say factors don't sneak in and cause stress for parents. You can do enough validating and nurturing as a parent and still feel overwhelmed with pressure as you parent.

Why?

Because parents are prone to fall into traps. You can be ensnared and not even realize it because the pattern is so ingrained in your brain. The most common traps for even the most dedicated parents are (1) *should* thinking, (2) *what-if* thinking, and (3) living one generation back.

These traps can cause more stress and pressure on you than your toddler's unexpected behaviors. They can hinder your relationship with your child too.

Stress Trap One: *Should* Thinking

The first trap is that of perfectionistic thinking, otherwise known as *should* thinking. Remember the second impossible mission we talked about discarding? *It's your job to make sure you do everything right (perfectly).*

This is where this trap is set. Before you dismiss the subject because you think you're not a perfectionist, read on. Perfectionism is more subtle than having things "just so," and it's not exposed by the neatness of your closet or work area. Perfectionistic thinking can be summed up in the word *should.* It's based on how you think things *should* be. Perfectionism includes deep-seated thinking patterns that hold a concise, rigid view of how things *should* be done in order to be right. Perfectionism means there's only one right way to do something and you *should* do it *that* particular way. Ever hear *should* statements from:

Parents or parents-in-law?
Moms who attend the same moms' group you attend?
Siblings?
Friends in your small group?

This perfectionistic thinking falls along a continuum. As you read this section, see if any of the thinking patterns fit you or someone you know. If so, ask yourself how *much* fits—a little, some, or a whole lot.

Do any of the following statements sound familiar?

- "Emmi, you *should* say hello whenever people greet you."
- "I *should* be a better parent."
- "I *shouldn't* have yelled at Missy that way."
- "You *shouldn't* get angry at your mother."
- "Josh, you *shouldn't* argue with me, ever."

Have you ever uttered statements like these?

While the statements wrapped around the *should* or *shouldn't* words sound good, even biblical at times, they are inherently dangerous to you and your preschooler for at least three reasons.

1. The Danger of Condemning Words

Perfectionism attempts to impose submission through condemnation and fear of condemnation.

How does this work?

A *should* statement will always be followed by a second statement—usually implied but not spoken aloud. It might sound something like this:

- "Emmi, you *should* say hello whenever people greet you . . . *but you didn't* (condemning tone)."
- "I *shouldn't* have yelled at Missy that way . . . *but I did.*"
- "You *shouldn't* get angry at your mother . . . *but you did.*"

47

- "Josh, you *shouldn't* ever argue with me . . . *but you are.*"
- "I *should* be a better parent . . . *but I'm not.*"

You probably never say the second half of the statement aloud, but it's still there. Can you hear it? Do you hear the condemnation? Do you feel your blood pressure going up? Does it sound very similar to somebody else's voice inside your head—a parent, an adult sibling, somebody on your block? If you want your life riddled with condemnation and/or contempt, that's your choice, but it's no way to be a healthy parent. Why condemn yourself? Why pass the condemnation on to your child?

2. The Danger of Giving Up Choices

Perfectionistic thinking contains a second danger. *Should* thinking leaves you—or the other person—with no viable options. You have to do things the *should* way or you're "wrong." You failed. You lost. You messed up. After all, you *should* do it the *should* way, *shouldn't* you?

If your choice is between *should* or *failure*, is that really much of a choice?

"Well, not really."

Exactly.

The power to influence has been snatched away from you, not by another person or a foreign army, but by your own unhealthy thinking pattern.

If your choice as a professional is between doing something the *should* way or being seen as *incompetent*, is that really a choice?

"No, I guess it isn't."

Do you hear the all-or-nothing, black-and-white thinking that accompanies *should* statements?

- When you have no choice, you have no control.
- When you have no control, you feel out of control.

Feel the stress building? Can you feel the pressure to do it right (i.e., perfectly—the *should* way)? This is where the urge originates to grab for whatever control you think you need to feel back in control.

Again, living without choices is no way to be free and no way to parent.

3. The Danger of Disallowing Healthy Pride

The final danger inherent in *should* thinking is that it prevents the experience of feeling healthy pride. In other words, when you do something well, with excellence, and get it "right," you don't get credit for it, because "After all, that's how you *should* have done it in the first place!"

Da dum pah. (That's the sound of a lead balloon rolling down the hallway.)

Get Free from Stress Trap One

There is something much more accurate than perfectionistic thinking. Again, let me generalize Jesus' statement "Then you will know the truth, and the truth will set you free." Perfectionistic thinking doesn't surrender easily. As humans, we're creatures of habit, especially in our thinking. But *should* thinking can be changed for the better. It's a matter of exchanging the lie for the truth.

The lie: "I *should* pray for my kids every morning." (You can already hear the second statement inside your head, can't you? Go ahead; say it out loud: "But I don't.")

The truth: "I *could* . . . I *would like to* . . . I *choose to* pray for my kids every morning, or as many mornings as I can."

Before you think I'm simply playing a psychological word game with you, check it out. Which statement is actually more *accurate*? Which statement is more *truthful*?

Quiz question: Where is it written that on this particular planet, in this particular millennium, on this specific continent, that this particular person (you) *should* pray for your child every day? Show me the law that says that.

Answer: There *isn't* a law that says that.

Which means there isn't a "right" time or place for prayer.

Which means you didn't break any law.

Which means you didn't do anything wrong.

Which means there's no reason to be condemned by others or by your own thinking.

Can you hear the difference underlying the actual English words?

I could—

I wish—

or *I choose*—

Joshua told the nation of Israel, "But if serving the Lord seems undesirable to you, then *choose for yourselves* this day whom you will serve, whether the gods your forefathers served beyond the River, or the gods of the Amorites, in whose land you are living" (Joshua 24:15, italics added).

Israel *could* choose:

- the God who brought them out of the land of Egypt and into the Promised Land (option one),
- *or* the gods of their ancestors beyond the Euphrates River (option two),
- *or* the gods of the Amorites (option three).

There was no "You *have to*—" or "You *should*—" from God.

There are no "You *should*" statements coming from God today—for you or for your preschooler. *Should* statements successfully steal the freedom and power that is truly yours—and your child's.

Joshua finished his presentation with a resounding, unashamed, free-will choice. He said, "But as for me and my household, we will [*choose* to] serve the LORD" (Joshua 24:15). Not "because we *should* serve God; after all, we are Israelites, so we *should*," but because "we *choose* to serve the LORD."

Almost sounds biblical, doesn't it? "There is now no condemnation for those who are in Christ Jesus" (Romans 8:1). That's an *every-day-of-our-lives* verse. God is saying that nobody, for any reason, at any time, has the permission, the position, or the power to judge or condemn you—including *you*.

Should statements condemn.

Should statements lie to you.

I wish statements free.

I could statements are true.

"So, what you're saying is I *could* have my devotions every morning. Or I *could* sleep in this morning (since I *was* up all night with a sick child and I don't want to get sick as well).

Or since I've never been a morning person, I *could* have my devotions after I get the kids out the door for playtime. *Or* I *could* rarely have devotions because life is so hectic right now. I'm really free to *choose?*"

That's *exactly* what I'm saying. Let go of the pressure.

"But I *want* to have my devotions. That's what *I want.* I *want* to obey God and devote myself and my day to Him. That's what *my heart* desires. It's *me.* So I'm going to try to have my devotions as many mornings as I can. Because I *want* to."

You got it! There's a *huge* difference between saying, "I want to have my devotions" and saying, "I should have my devotions." Hear it?

"I want to have my devotions" is a heartfelt statement of conviction and desire.

"I should have my devotions" comes from the trembling, cowering voice we read a few pages ago. Hear it? Feel it?

That's how truly powerful this thinking pattern is.

So when your discipline pays off and you *do* accomplish what you chose to do, you get the credit for it. You *can* feel a healthy, legitimate sense of pride, joy, and celebration. You accomplished your mission, because you *wanted* to, you *could* have, and you *chose* to see it through.

No *shoulds*—just choice and actions.

Let's Make a Deal

Here's an exercise that has worked for many of my clients. I call it "Let's Make a Deal." Pick a situation involving your child and your *should* thinking pattern and follow along.

Step 1. Take a sheet of paper and cut or tear it in half. On one piece of paper, write the words *should* and *shouldn't* in bold letters at the top. Below those words, write out the specific statement you say or think that has *should* or *shouldn't* in it. It would be something like, "Emmi, you should say hello whenever people greet you."

On the other sheet of paper, write the words *I could, I wish,* and *I choose* (again, in bold letters at the top). Below these statements, rewrite your own sentence using one of the phrases on this sheet. The example for Emmi's dad would be:

"*I want* (a form of *I wish*) you to say hello whenever people greet you."

Or, "Remember (a form of *choose*) to say hello whenever people greet you."

Step 2. Lay both pieces of paper in front of you, face up.

Step 3. Decide which set of words—which thinking pattern—you want to keep and live by.

"I know I *should* take the piece of paper with the *could* word, *shouldn't* I?"

You *could* choose the *could* paper or you *could* choose the *should* paper or you *could* ignore this exercise altogether.

"But I *should* choose the 'right' one, *shouldn't* I?" you might ask.

You have options, which mean you have choices, which means you have the right kind of control.

By the way, notice how good the *shoulds* keep sounding? Notice how sneaky they are too? I hope it helps you become more aware of just how subtle this kind of thinking is, and how common it can be personally and in our Christian communities.

So which piece of paper—which thinking pattern—are you going to *choose* to keep?

Step 4. Whichever piece of paper you choose to live by, keep. Be aware that whichever thinking pattern you discard, you can't think that way or speak that way anymore. Ever.

"I know I *shouldn't* say *should* anymore, but *what if* I say the words I *shouldn't* say?"

Again, see how sneaky the *should* thinking is? And how normal it sounds?

Step 5. If you chose the *could* paper, take the *should* piece of paper—along with your *should* sentence—and destroy it, rip it up, whatever. Just don't keep it around. If you decide to keep the *should* paper, it's your choice. You *chose* freely.

If you choose to keep the *could* paper, next comes the work part. Every time you have an opportunity to use *should* or *shouldn't*, stop yourself. Instead, use one of the *I could*, *I wish*, or *I choose* options. Use this on yourself, your spouse, your boss, and, of course, your preschooler. It will take conscious effort, especially at first, but ultimately it will be worth it. This change in thinking will take anywhere from a few weeks to several months. Be patient with yourself and keep working. This is the essence of how to go about being "transformed by the renewing of your mind," as Paul wrote in Romans 12:2. This is the way to get rid of undue parenting pressures, keep the control that is rightfully yours, and get out from under as much stress as possible.

A Practice Run

Okay, let's run through the five steps as a practice. Dad, you be Emmi's dad, Bill. (Mom, you can be Billie instead if you want.) Here we go.

First, can you hear the condemning tone when you say it this way?

·"Emmi, you *should* say hello whenever people greet you . . ."

Can you hear the second part of the sentence? It's there in some form or fashion.

". . . *but you didn't.*"

Here's the thing: You may not hear it, but rest assured your young child hears the condemnation—*senses* it is more like it. Is that what you want Emmi to pick up from you about her reluctance to say hello whenever people greet her?

"Not really."

Didn't think so.

Step 1. So do this. Take out a piece of paper and cut or tear it in half. On one piece of paper, write the words *should* and *shouldn't* in bold letters at the top. Below those words write the sentence "Emmi, you should say hello whenever people greet you."

If you want to use a real sentence you might use with your own child, do that. If you can't think of one right now, just use Bill's sentence.

On the second piece of paper, write the words *could, wish*, and *choose* (again, in bold letters at the top). Below these words, write both of these sentences:

"Emmi, I want you to say hello whenever people greet you."

"Emmi, remember to say hello whenever people greet you."

Step 2. Lay both pieces of paper in front of you, face up. Read each sentence below the words in bold. Be intentional and listen to the difference in the meanings, not just the words. If you're somewhere where you can read aloud and pretend the situation is actually happening right now, do so. You may find there's some emotion in the sentences you didn't realize was there. Take as much time with this step as you need to until you truly get the difference between the two ways of thinking and speaking.

Step 3. Decision time. Which set of words—which thinking pattern—do you want to keep and live by?

Your reaction might be "I never thought of it this way before. I don't want my child ever to feel I'm condemning her for anything. I just want her to learn social manners."

That's great, so learn to use wording that actually conveys what your heart intends to say, the *could, wish*, and *choose* words.

So which piece of paper—which set of words and thinking—do you want to keep and use from now on?

"The *could, wish*, and *choose* paper, of course!"

Great.

Step 4. From now on you can't say *should* or *shouldn't* anymore. That's the choice you just made. Follow me?

"I get it, but *what if* I *do* end up using *should* or *shouldn't* sometime?"

Relax. I realize your brain won't instantly make the change; that's completely normal. Whenever you find yourself thinking or saying *should* or *shouldn't*—whether you hear it immediately or even several hours later—practice Step 5: Relax (no pressure) and restate the sentence using *could, wish* (you can use *would like* or *want* as well), or *choose*. If you're somewhere where you can say the reworded sentence aloud, do so. If you can't, say it purposefully in your head.

That's all you need to do.

Depending on how deep the *should* ruts are in your brain, the *could* habit may take from one to three months to become your default thinking. That's okay; keep practicing and practicing and practicing. Your brain can—and will—make the change. It just will.

Are you sure you don't want to keep the *should* paper just in case?

"I'm sure!"

Great.

Some parents I was counseling a number of years ago were both seasoned experts at beating themselves and each other up with *should* statements. During one of our sessions, I played the "Let's Make a Deal" exercise with them. They *chose* to make the trade. In our next session they accused me of taking half their vocabulary away! Without the use of *should* or *shouldn't*, they found themselves speechless (which was very rare for them both). They admitted openly they didn't know how to talk to each other, their children, their friends, or anyone else. They were so used to the *should* mind-set that they had to restructure their entire vocabulary.

Ultimately, they both thanked me because not only did they feel less personally condemned, they also felt less condemned by each other. The atmosphere in their house finally felt free. In fact their normally clueless five-year-old son noticed and commented how much happier the house seemed to be. By example, their entire family learned to speak and think the "*could* way." In the end, the father, Gary, said: "It's made a huge difference throughout our whole house! Thank you."

Should thinking is the spawning ground for worry thinking. Welcome to Stress Trap Two.

Stress Trap Two: *What-if* Thinking

The second parenting trap involves another thinking pattern—that of worry. As I address the subject of worry, some basic definitions are critical. Here's your vocabulary lesson for the day:

fear \ f-'ear \ noun:
An intense emotional reaction to a legitimate, present danger.

anxiety \ ang 'zeye uh tee \ noun:
An intense emotional reaction, usually of dread, to a perceived, anticipated, or future danger.

worry \ 'were ee \ noun:
The "street" term for anxiety.

concern \ kon 'cern \ noun:
The "Christianized" translation of *anxiety*. Since we know we *shouldn't* worry, we change it to being

"concerned." But a horse by any other color is still a horse. True concern is to express care and interest.

panic \ 'pan ik \ noun:
An ill-advised behavioral reaction when one is overwhelmed by the emotion of fear or anxiety.

obsession \ obb 'sess shun \ noun:
A persistent, often unwanted flooding of thoughts (or thought pattern) that is very difficult or impossible to stop.

Obsessive compulsive disorder \ obb 'sess ive, kom 'pols ive dis 'or der\ noun:
A disorder where one attempts to stop or ease obsessive thinking (see above) by engaging in a repetitive behavior, such as hand washing, counting, double-checking everything, cleaning, reciting words or phrases over and over again, etc.

Anxiety shows itself in different ways. Here's a partial list:

- trembling or shaking
- excessive worrying
- restlessness, being "keyed up" or "on edge"
- being easily fatigued
- difficulties in concentrating
- sleep problems
- the need for a "plan A" and a "plan B" and more plans beyond that

- avoiding situations or decisions that one's unsure about
- feeling stuck and unable to make decisions without a lot of effort
- the fear of being wrong
- thinking, always thinking
- the need to know what is going to happen next
- feelings of impending failure or rejection
- excessive controlling behavior
- feeling out of control
- depression
- anger, often for no apparent reason

Like perfectionism, worry is a thinking pattern summed up in the phrase *what if?*

"*What if* Jack gets kicked out of Sunday school again?"

"*What if* Mary Beth doesn't get into the advanced reading group at day care?"

"*What if* we were too hard on Seth and he just quits trying anymore?"

"*What if? What if? Lions and tigers and bears! Oh my!*"

Or maybe the focus is on bigger worries.

"*What if* my ex manages to gain primary custody of my son?"

"*What if* my father-in-law inappropriately touches my daughter like he did his other granddaughter thirteen years ago?"

Can you hear the thinking pattern? Can you feel the tension and pressure building inside?

Try listing your own *what-ifs* regarding your parenting or your preschooler.

The problem with *what-if* thinking is your focus. Worry (anxiety) pulls your focus into the future and away from the present. Present-tense fear says: "The house *is* burning *now*. Run!" Worry, on the other hand, says: "*What if* the house starts to burn tonight (future) when we're all sleeping?" (But the house *isn't* burning right *now* and nobody's sleeping right *now* either.)

What if? Feel the stress that comes with trying to control something that doesn't even exist? Can you feel the urge to grab for control that you can't have? Pressure, pressure, and more pressure. And you know, many of the things we worry about never happen anyway.

"But *what if* it does happen?"

I hear you, and that's exactly what we're going to sort out when we discuss the difference between control and influence. Hang in here with me—we'll get there.

To make this discussion more concrete, I'll create an example that involves swimming, an activity many families with young children enjoy. First, I'll make three familiar categories:

PAST
PRESENT
FUTURE

Let's say you sign up your preschooler for swim lessons at the local pool. And of course, you decide to watch his first lesson.

Okay, your son is splashing in the water, buoyed by the hands of a capable instructor. You don't worry about him splashing around. If you were to worry, what would you worry about?

"My son going under and drowning, of course!"

Right. But is "going under and drowning" in the PAST, the PRESENT, or the FUTURE?

"Present?"

No. He's *not* under the water, nor is he drowning right *now*.

"I know, but *what if*?"

No, he's *not*. You're worried about the *possibility* your little boy *may* go under; you're worried about the *possibility* he may drown, which is in the FUTURE. Your focus is on the FUTURE. He's in the PRESENT, splashing around and having a grand old time, while your mind gets sucked into the scary, FUTURE *what-if* world.

"But *what if* he goes under?"

"*What if* the instructor's hand slips off and he drowns?"

"*What if*?"

Follow my reasoning carefully. The FUTURE doesn't exist. Right?

And you *know* all the FUTURE events and *know* he's going to go under. Do you know he's going to drown?

Again, the FUTURE does not exist. And what control do you have over things that don't even exist? None. Because the future doesn't exist, and you truly don't have any control over things that don't exist because that part of the universe *is* out of your ability to control.

So you'll feel out of control, even when he's fine. When

you worry, you surrender the control that *is* legitimately yours—what you are able to do right here and now—in the PRESENT.

No, don't do that.

Because your mind got sucked into the *what-if* black hole of the FUTURE rather than focusing on the PRESENT, your chances of being distracted from what's real skyrockets, and so does your blood pressure.

Let's keep going. Now, say your son does slip out of the instructor's hands and his head goes under the water. That's PRESENT tense. You don't worry about him going under now. If you were to worry, what would you worry about *now*?

"Him drowning!"

Right. And is "him drowning" in the PAST, the PRESENT, or the FUTURE?

"The future, but—"

Right.

"But *what if* he doesn't come back up in time? *What if* the instructor doesn't save him? *What if*?"

While your brain is running through all the *what-if* possibilities, you miss the opportunity to watch your son learn how to hold his breath and begin to swim. Really.

Now he's popped back up. You're not worried about drowning *now*. You may notice he's gasping, but you're not worried about your son going under or not coming up or drowning, are you? What would you worry about *now* if you were still worrying?

"*What if* he's hurt?"

"*What if* he hates me for making him do this?"

"*What if* he's emotionally injured for life?"

"*What if* it's my fault because I made him take lessons in the first place?"

"*What if* my wife yells at *me* for this?"

"*What if*?"

Do you see the pattern? Wherever you are (PRESENT), your mind moves into the *what-if* world of the FUTURE (which doesn't exist).

You may think worry keeps you in control because you'll be ready for whatever comes. But worry actually takes control away from you right now.

Stress, stress, pressure. Again, not good.

"But I'm a mom, and good moms *should* worry!"

No. Good moms *care* for their children. Caring is in the PRESENT, where you are in control and choose to do something without the pressure of *what-if* thinking looming over you.

"How can I stop the worry thinking? *What if* I can't stop worrying? I *should* stop worrying, *shouldn't* I?"

Did you hear it? Even talking about stopping *what-if* thinking can cause some worry about not being able to stop it because *should* thinking says that's the "right" way to do it.

Hang in there. Your brain will make the changes; it'll just take time. Be patient with yourself.

By the way, I know these *should* and *what-if* thinking patterns very well. I'm a recovering perfectionist and worrier. When I became aware of my own *what-if* thinking running through my mind from morning until late at night, I began to ask around for ideas on how to stop the craziness inside my head. I got the standard clichés:

- "Just don't worry about tomorrow."
- "Take every thought captive . . ."
- "Just think about good things."

These answers represent the standard responses people throw at anxiety in an attempt to make it go away. I wasn't being sarcastic, but I would often respond with an honest "How?" All I got back then were blank looks, but no answers. Nobody could tell me *how* to shut down the *what-if* thinking pattern in my head. So I went searching desperately for something to help.

Get Free from Stress Trap Two

Breaking the *what-if* thinking pattern is similar to breaking the *should* thinking habit. You first have to identify the *what-if* thinking. Next, you stop that "record"—that thinking pattern—and replace it with the thinking pattern you *want* to have.

To help in this brain transition, I pieced together the following four-question technique. This technique is rather silly, yet it works. I've been teaching anxiety-prone clients this technique for many years now, and it works. It really does.

Put the following list of actions on a three-by-five-inch card:

1. Name five colors I see right now.
2. Name five sounds I hear right now (give yourself permission to create sounds as well, like scratching on the chair armrest, etc.).

3. Name five things I physically feel right now (not emotions, but things like "my watch on my wrist" or "wind in my hair," etc.).
4. Name something I need to be doing—or thinking about—*right now*.

Since worry is a bad thinking habit, you need to get the bad "record" out of your "jukebox" by creating a good thinking habit, a new record to take its place. Habits are built by repetition, so here you go.

Place the card by your nightstand. Tomorrow when you wake up, go over the four questions one at a time. You want to get your brain going in a new direction first thing in the morning. Whenever you can, ask and answer the questions out loud to yourself, even if you do it very quietly.

When you get up tomorrow, name five colors you see. Then name five sounds you hear and five things you physically feel.

Ask yourself, "What's the first thing I need to do after my feet hit the floor?" Go to the bathroom? Put your robe on and make the coffee? What?

Can you handle that? I'm sure you can, since you've been doing it for some time now. So do it.

What you *can't* do is make the coffee and handle the rest of the day right now, because the "rest of the day" isn't *here* in the PRESENT. The whole day is still in the FUTURE. Don't get sucked into *what-if* thinking about the day. *Just make the coffee.* Now, what's the *next* thing you need to do *right now*?

You see, moments are like snowflakes. One snowflake looks cute and pretty. A billion snowflakes equal a blizzard and can kill you. You *can* handle this moment. What you *can't* handle is this moment (while you make the coffee) *and* all the unknown snowflakes of the FUTURE all together. It's a blizzard in your brain.

This doesn't mean that the plans you make aren't good or necessary. But you can't *live* in the FUTURE with your body or your mind. Making plans happens in the PRESENT.

What's the difference between worrywart, *what-if* thinking and proactive behavior as a responsible parent?

What-if thinking is an attempt to live in the FUTURE, which we all know doesn't exist. Proactive behavior, on the other hand, is what concerned parents engage in—in the PRESENT.

> **proactive** \ pro 'ak tive \ adjective:
> Taking positive action now in order to prevent a negative outcome now and later.

As a proactive parent you *will* childproof your home (PRESENT-tense action) with things such as electrical outlet covers, door locks, doorknob covers, and cabinet security catches. This type of activity doesn't mean you are a worrywart. You're being a smart, action-oriented, responsible parent. That's very different from being a worrywart. Hear it?

These proactive plans make your house child-safe now (PRESENT) and will pay off in the FUTURE as well.

Plans like these will pay off in the FUTURE. But only when the FUTURE turns into the PRESENT and becomes real—which isn't right now.

Habits are built on repetition. Take your card with you,

have a second card for your organizer, put a card in your purse or briefcase, or log the questions into your smart phone. Three to five times during the day, review the four questions. It doesn't matter when, or what your circumstances are. If you can avoid getting carried away in a straitjacket, practice the technique out loud. When you find yourself involved in *what-if* thinking, answer the four questions again and again. Habits are built on repetition, and bad habits are broken the same way.

Practice. Practice. Practice.

Lastly, as you get ready for bed at night, repeat the four-question technique one final time. It's amazing how it can be Wednesday night, and you're already worrying about Thursday or Friday. And it's not even Thursday yet. Stay in Wednesday. Count sheep. Dream about your vacation in the Bahamas—or your backyard. Stay in the PRESENT. Enjoy going to bed rather than worrying about whether you'll be rested up for that important meeting you have tomorrow. One snowflake at a time.

When you use this little technique, some days you will win—successfully stopping the onslaught of *what-ifs*. Other days, *what-if* thinking will win. Over the period of time it takes to break a bad habit and make a new habit, the *what-is* (PRESENT) will take root. In the course of two to three months, the change will happen. Not only will the *what-is* take root and become your default thinking, the *what-if* thinking will fade into the background.

What-if thinking may sneak in from time to time, but not nearly as often. And if or when it does, *what-if* thinking will feel like a foreigner.

Here's why and how this technique works. Questions one through three use your physical senses to bring your focus out of the FUTURE and into the PRESENT. Colors, sounds, and physical touches are in the PRESENT realm only. It's a way of getting your mind to think deliberately about what's around you *right now*. And if you're thinking about what's around you in the PRESENT, you're not thinking of all the *what-ifs* of the FUTURE. In the counseling world we call this a grounding technique.

Each question requires five responses so you can keep track on your fingers. That's as scientific as it gets.

People tend to believe that whatever they're thinking about is what they *should* be thinking about. If that were true, your mind would be like a Saint Bernard dog taking *you* for a walk, jerking you into the bushes (*what if*) then off toward a tree (*what if*) and wherever it randomly wants to go. Your wandering thoughts dictate what you think about, not you. Wouldn't the walk be a whole lot better if *you* tell the Saint Bernard where *you* are going and make the dog heel and follow *you*? Who's in control here, you or the dog? Who's in control here, you or the worry thinking? Herein rests the importance of the fourth question.

When you answer the question *What do I need to do or think about right now? you* are choosing what *you* think about in the PRESENT, and *you* are in charge and have the control—the right kind of control. If you need to study, then study. If you want to take a morning shower, take a shower. If you're driving, then drive and enjoy the drive. Relax your brain and stay in the PRESENT moment only. Think about *what is*.

As many times as I've seen this happen, I still see the park in Manitou Springs, Colorado, where we used to swing our girls. A mom was pushing her preschool-aged daughter on the swing while talking endlessly on her cell phone. For some reason, this example sticks more deeply in my memory than all the others I've witnessed.

No! Don't do that. Your young child can sense your absence. This mom was "not there" in the park; she was somewhere else. She was *not* spending time with her daughter even though she thought she was. Not really.

If you're pushing your daughter in a swing, *be there*. Push the swing *only*. Make sure you are completely *there*. If you're playing Legos with your son, *be there*. Play Legos *only*. Make sure your mind and attention are in the same place as your body.

Don't believe your preschooler "picks up" on it? Think again. How do you like it when you're talking with someone who's also on his or her cell phone talking with somebody else? How do you like it when that person in the meeting you called has that "checked-out" look on his or her face? Do you notice it?

Remember, young children sense, perceive, and pick up on behaviors more than you think, even more than they cognitively comprehend.

Be *there*.
Be *all* there.
Be all there *only*.

Stress Trap Three: Living One Generation Back

The final stress trap worth noting is often labeled by therapists as "living one generation back." To see if you tend to do this, consider the statements below. Have you ever made them or others like them?

- "I'll never be gone as much as my father was."
- "I resent my mother. She was too strict. She suffocated my brother and me. I'm never going to try to run my kids' lives."
- "I never got to play baseball because the games were always on Sunday, and Dad didn't believe in 'working' on 'the Lord's Day.' My kids are going to be able to play baseball, even if the games are on Sunday."

Those attitudes and decisions are prompted by parents who are living *their* lives (trying to repair or undo their own hurts) through the lives of their children.

Most of the time, parents do this unknowingly and unintentionally. It's not a conscious choice, but we can do it nonetheless. In the end, it tempts you to overcontrol situations, events, your spouse, and your preschooler.

P.S. It doesn't work for your spouse, you, or your preschooler.

Get Free from Stress Trap Three

It's wise to learn from the past—mistakes and successes. Be careful you're not trying to "fix" *your* past by living through your *child's* present.

71

We have hopes, dreams, expectations, and desires for our kids. That's normal and healthy. But if not kept in check, those dreams and expectations can also become a trap when we hold on to them too tightly and attempt to fit reality—in the form of our children—into our expectations.

Remember Jennifer (chapter 1), trying to live out her dreams through her daughter? It didn't work for Jennifer. It doesn't work for you. It won't work for your child either.

Don't live one generation back.

Don't parent one generation back, either.

Thinking a New Way

Do any of these stress traps sound familiar to you? Do you think they may fit your spouse? If so, be careful to "take the beam out of your own eye" before trying to help your spouse with the speck in his or hers. Giving—and receiving—good counsel can be appropriate when team parenting.

If you find any of these types of thinking patterns in your life, I'd encourage you to spend as much time here as you need to—or come back to this chapter once you finish the book. Work on what fits, and leave the rest for other parents to deal with. Staying out of these traps makes the job of parenting significantly less stressful.

If you don't find yourself falling into any of these traps, great! While it's important to realize the traps that get you into a tizzy, it's just as important to realize you're doing things correctly and *not* falling into the stress traps that make your parenting job harder. Good job. Keep going. And relax.

Low-Pressure Principle 2

• • • • • • • •

MAKE FRIENDS WITH
FREE WILL

FIVE

THE GIFT OF FREE WILL

I OVERHEARD THE following conversation in a restaurant not long ago.

> PARENT: "Missy, tell the waitress what you want to eat from the kiddy menu."
> MISSY: "I want a corn dog!"
> PARENT: "You don't want a corn dog. You don't even know what a corn dog is."
> MISSY: "I want a corn dog!"
> PARENT: "No, you don't want a corn dog. You ordered mac and cheese last time, and that's what you want this time, too. Remember?"

MISSY: "I want a corn dog!"

PARENT (turning to the server): "She'll have macaroni and cheese."

It's a familiar story: A preschooler's *free will* ends where a parent's begins. But is that how it has to be?

Even though I'm ordained as a minister, I promise this chapter won't turn into a theological primer on the difference between God's sovereignty and our human free will. Allow me, though, to start with three simple questions.

Imagine the following dialogue between a Theology 101 student and the class professor.

STUDENT: "God is sovereign, right?"

PROFESSOR: "You are correct."

STUDENT: "Didn't God give human beings a free will?"

PROFESSOR: "He most certainly did."

STUDENT: "Well, then how does God orchestrate these seemingly opposing concepts?"

PROFESSOR: "As theologians we don't know. What we *do* know is He is God, and He balances these two realities very well."

What this discussion boils down to practically is that you and I make choices every day—as does your preschooler—as we live under the umbrella of God's continual and constant sovereignty.

Let's revisit the Garden of Eden.

Then God said, "Let us make man in our image, in
our likeness, and let them rule over the fish of the
sea and the birds of the air, over the livestock, over
all the earth, and over all the creatures that move
along the ground." So God created man in his own
image, in the image of God he created him; male
and female he created them.

(GENESIS 1:26-27)

The LORD God took the man and put him in the
Garden of Eden to work it and take care of it. And
the LORD God commanded the man, "You are free
to eat from any tree in the garden; but you must not
eat from the tree of the knowledge of good and evil,
for when you eat of it you will surely die."

(GENESIS 2:15-17)

We know Adam and Eve were created as perfect beings
and placed in a perfect environment.

We know there was a rule: "Don't eat of that tree." We
know God was—and still is—sovereign, all-knowing, and
ever present. We also know Adam and Eve made the choice
to eat the forbidden fruit.

Follow me carefully now.

On that specific day, described in Genesis chapter 3, God
watches Adam and Eve walk toward the forbidden tree. He
hears them talking about the fruit. He understands what they
are about to do. He knows the serpent is laying a trap for the
entire human race.

Does He stop them?

No.

Why not? Why didn't God jump out and stop Adam and Eve? Why didn't He ask Adam, "What have we talked about before?" Or just say "Stop!"? Why didn't God stop them? Didn't He know what the consequences were? Didn't He care? Why?

This isn't something to be taken lightly, even if you're not a student of theology. Look at the consequences of that choice. Human beings die—or will die—because of that one choice. God the Father chose to sacrifice His own Son, Jesus, to redeem humanity, all because of that single choice described in Genesis chapter 3.

So *why* didn't He? Every person is made in God's image. A piece of that image God placed in us is the ability to freely choose; we have free will. We are free moral agents.

If God had stopped Adam and Eve, He would have essentially taken that piece of His very image out of them. Humanity would then have forevermore followed God—not out of free will as human beings, but by default as human robots.

No other option means no choice.

No choice means no free will.

God refused to do that to His human race, so He let Adam and Eve exercise their free will and choose—and choose *wrongly*.

For the record, God did not *make* Adam and Eve choose wrongly. He did not *desire* them to do so. However—in His sovereignty—He *allowed* them to choose for themselves.

In addition, notice the absence of statements like "Adam, you *shouldn't* . . ." or "You guys *should* . . ." God didn't manage Adam and Eve with *should* statements. He didn't handle the nation of Israel (Joshua 24:15) with *should* statements. He doesn't approach you or me today with *should* statements. It's good to hear this again, even though we've already discussed this.

Your Child Has Free Will Too

In case you haven't figured it out yet, God gave that same free will to your preschooler. She has a free will to make good choices—or bad ones.

"But I don't *want* her to make bad choices!" you say.

I understand.

However, she has the God-given gift to choose either way. In the end, the choice is truly hers. And it's a gift, a very valuable gift.

This wild card comes up any time we get into a conversation about what a mom or dad *should* do in order to be a good parent. It's generally a slippery slope into the subject of control. If you try to override your child's free will, whether by threatening, begging, or using guilt tactics (read: *should, shouldn't,* and more *should* statements), you actively manipulate—you coerce—your preschooler into behaving according to *your* will.

Does Missy's story at the start of this chapter sound okay to you? Whose will wins out in the corn dog debate? It may sound like it's no big deal to you as a parent—because *the parent's* will prevailed. But the parent still overrode the daughter's will and choice. That's manipulation.

God didn't—and won't—manipulate. When you

manipulate your child's will, you're trying to take that special piece of God's image out of your child. It won't work, so don't try. It's also wrong. Besides, none of us likes being the target of manipulation, no matter our age. That goes for two- and three-year-olds as well as you and me.

Parents who understand low-pressure parenting know the difference between *control* and *influence*. Short and crisp. No, you *don't* have *control* over your preschooler's thoughts or behaviors. What you *do* have is considerable *influencing* power over him and his specific circumstances. We'll address the difference between control and influence in chapters 7 and 8.

Don't hurry through this very important concept of free will. It's crucial to grasp its significance.

Several years ago I saw a bumper sticker that I wish I had today:

PEOPLE HAVE THE RIGHT TO BE STUPID

The words are plain, simple, blunt—and very true.

"So what's a parent to do? Give up? Let my kid lie right to my face or make life-threatening mistakes like poking a stick into a hornets' nest? What's a parent to do?"

In all my years of working with people, I've simplified life into what I call the "Three Rules of Life." These aren't children's rules. These aren't "Ma and Pa" rules. If you're a human being—and breathing—these rules are for you. On the surface, these rules may appear simplistic. They aren't, and they're a great place to start.

Rule One: You Live and Die by Your Own Choices

You live and die by your own choices. Fortunately, most of the choices your preschooler or toddler faces are not actual life-or-death choices.

Yes, people influence us. Yes, circumstances affect us greatly. Yes, things happen every day that we don't have control over. But we *do* have control over the choices we make in *response* to those circumstances and people. We all have our free will, and our lives move in the direction of either life or death with every choice we make. This begins as soon as your toddler learns to say no.

It amazes me how human beings seem to comprehend Rule One at a very young age.

This rule may be scary for us as parents because we must face the reality that we have less control over our young child and his or her circumstances than we would like. Don't fret; Rules Two and Three are coming.

Rule Two: You Can Choose "Smart" or Choose "Stupid"

Since you live and die by your choices (Rule One), *you can choose "smart" or choose "stupid."* Some choices are also legal versus illegal or moral versus immoral. But all choices boil down to this basic question: "With this choice of yours, *are you going to choose smart or stupid?*" Blunt—and true.

If Rule One perked some ears, Rule Two can get almost any discussion going hot and heavy. Human beings are very versed at using *should* statements, judging others, and making rules for others to follow.

Why?

It's often to bring some semblance—so we presume—of control (*our* control, *our* way, and generally for *our own* benefit). As we talked about earlier, this is why parents' job descriptions are so out of sorts. Everyone has his or her own opinion of what *should* be on the smart list and what *should* be on the stupid list.

Yes, you're entitled to your opinions, but you don't get to choose which actions and behaviors go on the stupid list or which go on the smart list. I will quickly admit, I don't choose which actions and behaviors go on which list either—even being the author of this parenting book.

The smart list and stupid list have been predetermined for all of us first by God's Word and second by society—in that order. They were here before you and I were born. Both lists will be here long after we are gone. No human "owns" the

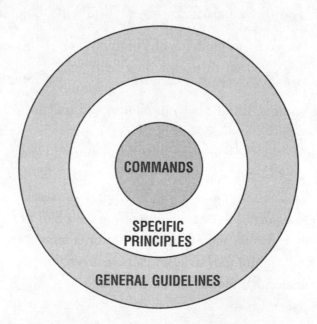

lists, so there's no human—alive or dead—who has power or authority to make or change the lists. This is why knowing and understanding as much of the Bible as you possibly can is so important.

To help you visualize, I'll employ the image of an archery target with three rings. I use this frequently with my clients when we want to know what Scripture says about a particular subject.

1. Direct Commands

We start with the bull's-eye—the innermost ring—and ask the question "Are there any *direct commands* in Scripture (clear, specific statements of "do this" or "don't do that") that speak to this situation?"

If there is a *direct command* regarding the issue, *obey the command!* It's as simple as that. Don't argue, just do it. These commands are line items on the smart list.

When there is a *direct command*, and you choose to disobey, you break the law—a civil law or one of God's moral laws.

When you break a law, you commit a crime.

With every crime there is a specific punishment.

This inner circle is where true right or wrong exists.

Choosing to obey the command is right—or smart.

Choosing to disobey the command is wrong—or stupid.

Simple as that.

Some individuals, leaders, authors, speakers, or organizations in Christian circles tend to force *all* of Scripture's statements into the bull's-eye circle. To be blunt, this is an attempt to manipulate others by making everything a *should* or *shouldn't* statement. If God's name is stamped on it, it sounds more "official" and who can argue?

When you try to live this way, you feel a demand to give more than there is of you to give. This results in pressure, false guilt, doubt, stress—you get the idea.

When you try to turn the whole of life into a set of do's and don'ts—rights or wrongs, *shoulds* or *shouldn'ts*—you set yourself up for failure, or pride and "humble arrogance."

That's not good at all—for anyone. Please be discerning.

Back in 1996, I took my family—my wife, Becky, our thirteen-year-old daughter, Terryll, and our eleven-year-old daughter, Heidi—to climb Mount Sherman. Mount Sherman is known as one of the easier "fourteeners" (peaks over 14,000 feet in elevation) in Colorado. It's a great introduction into the art of climbing, and that June there was still a significant amount of snow on the peak. I told the girls about the route and conditions, and suggested things to wear and take along. We also talked about the weather patterns for the Colorado Rocky Mountains, even though I didn't expect them to keep track of the current weather. That's what they got for having a "mountain guide" for a dad.

Both girls chose to wear shorts.

Test Question One: Are there any *direct commands* that say, "Thou shalt not let thy daughters wear shorts to climb a fourteener"?

Answer: No.

Okay then, let's keep going.

2. Specific Principles

Back to the target illustration. If there's *not* a direct command, then move to the next ring out and ask the question "Are there any *specific principles* mentioned in Scripture that address this topic?"

If there are *specific principles* that speak to this issue, *then apply those principles as clearly as you understand them.* These things are also on the smart list. Realize, though, that *specific principles* allow room for differences in the application of those principles.

Back to the bull's-eye diagram. If my arrow lands an inch to the left of the center ring, and yours hits an inch below the center ring, who's wrong? Who "missed the mark"?

"Nobody," you might guess.

Exactly.

We're *both* in the second ring—just in different locations. We're *both* applying the *specific principles* the best we can understand them. We just didn't apply them in exactly the same way. Here, in the arena of principles and their application, is where the body of Christ allows for differences.

It's very important to note that *specific principles* are not laws (commands).

Therefore, there's no law to break.

So neither of us broke a law.

So neither of us did anything wrong.

When it comes to applying principles, we can be smart or stupid, wise or foolish. Still, neither one of us broke a law, so neither is doing anything wrong.

Back to the family climb. Are there any *specific principles* that speak to allowing your daughters to wear shorts when mountain climbing? Careful now. Read it correctly. We're not talking about specific principles that address safety; we're looking for *specific principles* addressing my decision as a father to allow them to wear shorts.

Are there any *specific principles* that speak to this?

"No. But *shouldn't* you have made them wear long pants? Isn't that what a good father *should* do?"

Those *should* statements raise their heads all the time, don't they? And those statements sound so natural and true. But they're not true.

So are there any *specific principles* that speak to this?

"Well, no," you say with some hesitation. "But *shouldn't* you have made—"

Slow down. Are you saying there are *specific principles* that speak to fathers about allowing daughters to wear shorts when climbing a mountain? Is that what you're saying?

"No, I guess not."

Back to the bull's-eye diagram. If there are *specific principles* addressing the issue at hand, apply the principle or principles as best you can. When it comes to applying specific principles, there can be a wise or foolish nature to them.

Test Question Two: Are there any *specific principles* that address the situation of a father making his daughters wear long pants on a climb?

"No, but *I* wouldn't—"

Are you saying I made a stupid choice and your choice is the right choice? Let's ask, "Am I caring for my daughters?" The answer should be yes.

3. General Guidelines

Finally, if there are no *direct commands* and no *specific principles addressing a particular issue*, then move to the target's outside ring. The question to ask the Scriptures now is "Are there any *general guidelines* that speak to the topic at hand?" This ring allows us the most room to express our free will and to be different from each other as we each strive to live out the guidelines, teachings, and encouragements found in the Bible.

I'll say it again: We are all entitled to our own personal beliefs, opinions, and ways of applying biblical principles. Not all of life is black and white, right or wrong. Yes, there *are* the bull's-eye parts of life. There *are* commands laid out in the Scriptures, though there are fewer commands than some of us as parents would like to acknowledge.

Natural consequences play a big role as well. Jumping out the window might seem great and exciting to a four-year-old child who wants to fly through the air with Peter Pan and Wendy, but the law of gravity puts such a choice on the stupid list. Every time.

Your preschooler doesn't get to say what goes on each list either. She does, however, get to choose between the behaviors and actions on the smart list and those on the stupid list. It is her choice to make.

"What about your daughters wearing shorts to hike a fourteener?"

Test Question Three: Are there any *general guidelines* that speak to a father's allowing his daughters to wear shorts when climbing?

"No."

That's right. Now, are there any *general guidelines* that speak to a father's interactions with his daughters and the importance of keeping his daughters safe?

Yes! Many of them. They are, however, only guidelines—not laws or specific principles.

Woven into validating and nurturing your preschooler will be multiple moments to teach which actions and attitudes are on which list. *Children don't know the lists.* As you *validate* and *nurture*, you impart these lists accurately to them through words, examples, and correction.

Children don't know the lists. So you may have a son who (a) truly believes he *can* fly like Superman, and (b) is impulsive enough to actually try. Before he jumps off the stairwell banister and "learns the hard way," explain to him the facts about human limitations, gravity, and flying. Show him he can't actually fly. If he insists, go ahead and let him "try" to fly—over your queen-size bed, that is. Natural consequences will clearly show themselves, but without any physical harm to his body. And if by chance he inherited a streak of stubbornness from you, let him try (still over your bed) again and again until he does learn. Learning the hard way doesn't have to be the same as learning the painful way.

That's a relief, isn't it?

What about my daughters? In my pack I carried extra clothes I might have needed on the climb as well as extra clothing for my daughters. As it turned out, Becky and Terryll turned around at about the 12,500-foot elevation mark. They returned to the vehicle safe, sound, warm, and content with their choice.

Terryll chose to wear shorts. She chose to turn around. And she was content with her choices and learned a lot in the process.

Heidi chose to go on up the mountain. And she got cold.

She chose to accept a hat I was carrying (for a situation just like this).

Later, she chose to accept a sweatshirt I was carrying.

Later, she chose to accept a jacket I brought.

And she chose to keep going.

Heidi and I made the 14,036-foot summit, even with a strong wind that would have actually blown her off the summit ridge had I not held on to her. We made it back to the vehicle. Heidi was content with her choices and learned a lot in the process.

Last Test Question: So as far as *general guidelines* on fathering, did I take care of my daughters? Did I allow my daughters to exercise their free will? Did I provide for their needs? Did I keep my daughters safe? Were they validated and nurtured?

Yes to all. Again, maybe you would do it very differently with your daughters, and that's okay.

All of that was a part of Rule Two.

Rule Three: Somebody or Something Will Make Your Life Miserable When You Choose "Stupid"

Call it "cause and effect" or "reap what you sow"—it's true all the same. When you choose "stupid," eventually that choice will come back around and bite you. There's always an "ouch" to a stupid choice. So it is here—with Rule Three—where parental *influencing* springs to life.

When your preschooler chooses "smart," tell her so. By doing this you teach her what's on the smart list (a list she's just learning). She also reaps the rewards—whether that is a bedtime story, a cookie, or a smile from her dad. Remind her of this too. *Connect smart choices with positive outcomes.*

When she chooses stupid, she reaps the "ouch," and tell her this too. Teach her what's on the stupid list (again, she's just learning this list). This "ouch" might be not getting a cookie, a time-out, correction, or even some form of punishment. Be sure to take time to teach her what's on the smart list for next time.

Depending on your preschooler's temperament, connecting the negative consequence back to her wrong or foolish choice may come immediately—if she can make the connection then—or after the emotions calm down and the dust has settled.

Just for a reference point, you'll likely be linking the cause with the effect (good or bad) somewhere in the neighborhood of a million times before your preschooler actually gets it. Don't be hard on yourself if you say things over and over again. Relax, that's normal.

While you can't *make your child turn out right* (that's not your job, remember), it *is* your job to reward smart choices and give consequences for stupid ones. That's just the way the world goes around. That's life. That's *influencing* your child.

That's healthy, influencing, low-pressure parenting right there.

The Three Rules Lived Out

Let me use this same story of my family's climbing excursion to illustrate how my daughters interacted with the Three Rules of Life.

My daughters each made their own choices. Nobody made their choices for them—including me. They lived by their own choices. Rule One is alive.

Both of them made a stupid choice (not wrong) to wear shorts. Yet both of them made *many* smart choices throughout the entire day. Rule Two.

My girls felt the negative impact (the "ouch") of their foolish choice; they got cold. Terryll reaped the benefit of a smart choice to turn around and go back to the comfort and warmth of our vehicle. Heidi reaped the benefit of a number of smart choices to accept clothing from me and later reached the summit. She also got the benefit—eventually—of the vehicle's comfort. Rule Three.

This particular story is fresh on my mind as I write this chapter, because Heidi reminded me of that (now wonderful) "learning experience" as we celebrated Father's Day. It's a lesson she learned nineteen years ago, still vividly remembers, and uses today as an adult.

"Oh boy, *do* I remember that lesson!"

Terryll commented that the pattern of making her own choices and living with the consequences has become so ingrained that she finds it challenging *not* to think in those terms. She added, "And to this day, I have no regrets about turning around and heading for the car."

Smart girls—adult women, I mean. And yes, I am completely biased!

How Much Free Rein?

"Just how much safety and responsibility do I need to maintain and still give my child his free will to choose?"

This may be the hardest decision for a parent to make because it's an awkward balancing act between exercising my responsibility as the parent and (as the responsible parent) allowing my daughter liberty to exert that free will of hers.

Especially if she might get hurt somehow.

"The Two Kinds of Pain"

In an effort to keep things simple and understandable, I've divided pain into two major kinds.

1. Pain that hurts because it hurts—but there's no damage.

This is the kind of pain Heidi felt from her DTaP shot. This is the kind of pain your son feels when he's teething, has the chicken pox, or gets a splinter in his finger. This is the kind of pain your daughter feels when the head of her favorite doll falls off or her best friend can't come over to play. It hurts—physically, emotionally, or relationally—but that's it.

2. Pain that hurts because damage or destruction is happening.

This is the kind of pain you need to address *right away*, intervening on your preschooler's behalf to stop the damage and/or destruction.

I just talked with a dad whose preschool-aged son broke his arm falling off the slide in their backyard. The pain from a broken bone is pain because there's *damage* happening to the body. The dad was smart to stabilize his son's arm and drive him to the emergency room right away.

The old adage "Sticks and stones may break my bones, but words will never hurt me" is not true—especially for children. If someone came up to you today and told you, "You're ugly," would that create some small amount of emotional *pain*?

"Maybe—depending on who said it."

Would it *damage* or *destroy* you?

"No."

Exactly.

But those same words, "You're ugly," repeated often enough to a child, can actually *damage* that child's sense of self and personality. The lesson here: What may *not* cause damage to you, as an adult, may indeed cause damage to your preschooler. Having to put the family dog down may hurt you with the first kind of pain, but it could emotionally hurt your preschooler, and telling him to just get over it can result in the second kind of pain. Not a guarantee, just something to remember.

Life is full of the first kind of pain. And while that pain is real and can be quite intense, we don't need to fear or worry about that kind of pain.

"But I don't *want* my child to *ever* get hurt!"

I hear you.

"And, besides, what kind of parent would allow his or her child to be hurt in the first place?"

Was I a bad parent because I took Heidi to get her painful immunization shots? No. Not all pain can be avoided. On the other hand, if you *wanted* your preschooler to be hurt, you'd be a strange parent! Still, we don't need to fear the first kind of pain.

By the way, when I allowed my daughters their free-will decision to wear shorts for the climbing trip, I knew:

- that choice could possibly cause some hurt—the it-just-hurts kind of pain
- that choice would not be costly to their lives or leave them with any permanent damage of some sort—the destructive kind of pain

I also knew my daughters well enough to know they were ready for such a free choice. I would *not* have given the same free-will choice to them if they were ages one and two!

Yes, It's a Little Scary, But . . .

As parents, this is a part of life we need to accept. The Three Rules of Life are true; they are real. The good news is we already threw out those impossible jobs: *make them turn out right* and *make sure you do everything right (perfectly)*. Remember?

You don't have as much control as you would like to have. Your child does have the power to choose life or death, smart or stupid, right or wrong. And that can be very scary for a parent, I agree.

So take a deep breath, and embrace the reality that

whatever we do as parents—and how we do things as parents—there is this wild card called *free will.*

You can do everything right as a parent (not perfectly, mind you, but good enough), and your child can *still* choose stupid.

That part is *not* your fault. Yes, it breaks your heart, but it's *not* your fault.

I have worked with many parents who did things right, only to watch their children grow up and go the way of stupid choices. How many nights do you think the father of the Prodigal Son laid his head on the pillow with a knot in his stomach and an ache in his heart? (Read his story in Luke 15:11–32.)

I frequently tell clients, "When you fight reality, you lose." The same is true in parenting. Accept the reality of your preschooler's free will. Accept it as a *gift* from God. Accept—and then use—the Three Rules of Life.

Let's review. What's *not* your job?

"To make them turn out right and make sure I do everything right (perfectly)."

Right. What *is* your job?

"To *validate* and to *nurture.*"

Exactly. By doing so, you'll feel the demands and pressures of *should* thinking lighten and your job description shorten—even while accepting the truth that your preschooler has free will.

"About time I got some good news."

Amen to that!

SIX

GIVING THEM A VOICE

"Do you want to wear your snow boots (yay, snow boots!) or your tennis shoes to church today?"

Even in the middle of a Colorado winter we gave Terryll, then three years old, a choice—a voice—as to what footwear she wanted to wear. Heidi was only twelve months old, and she didn't get to choose her footwear—yet.

"What? You let your toddler pick what *she* wanted to wear in the middle of winter? Are you out of your mind?! You *should* make her wear the snow boots and be done with it. That's what any 'responsible' parent would do." These are common responses.

Let's slow down. Hear the pressure of others' voices and

the *should* statements wrapped in these reactions? Stress Trap One is a very tricky trap indeed.

Giving our daughter a voice was necessary to help develop her sense of self and an understanding of her gift of free will (chapter 5). It also gave her an opportunity to learn how to use her voice wisely.

Voiceless Is Dangerous

Why is giving your child a voice so important? Here's a very brief explanation:

- A child who grows up without a voice becomes a voiceless adult.
- A voiceless adult lacks (healthy) boundaries.
- An adult who lacks boundaries is a prime target for manipulation and/or abuse.

Not good at all. And sadly, I see way too many of this kind of adult in my practice.

Mary is one of those adults. She came to my practice complaining of depression, poor relationships with men, and panic attacks. She was a preacher's kid, and her "jukebox" was full of "records" like these:

- "Children are to be seen, not heard."
- "Always obey those in authority."
- "Always obey your elders."
- "Never talk badly about anyone."

She recounted many instances in her childhood when she was scared, sick, or upset, and her parents "shushed" her, saying, "Stop complaining. Don't you know others in the world have it much worse than you?" Mary's unconscious conclusions to all this were "Do what others say; don't challenge anyone ever" and "I don't have a voice."

Fast forward twenty-plus years. Mary was seeing her church's associate pastor for some spiritual direction in her life. Over several meetings, this pastor made sexual advances toward her and eventually began raping her.

Any guesses about what Mary's response was?

Nothing.

She didn't resist (*"Always* obey those in authority").

She didn't tell anybody about the rape (*"Never* talk badly about anyone").

She didn't voice her complaint to anyone ("Be seen, not heard").

Mary had been in therapy for years—yes, years—before coming to see me, and she was with me for some time before she finally gained her voice and verbalized the multiple rape incidents and the horror she experienced. She was middle-aged by this time. I was the first person she voiced these terrible experiences to—after more than twenty years of silent suffering.

Again, a child who grows up without a voice becomes a voiceless adult. A voiceless adult lacks (healthy) boundaries. An adult who lacks boundaries is a prime target for manipulation and/or abuse.

Not good at all.

Autonomy

During the preschool years, two developmental stages need to be successfully addressed. During one of these stages, from about twelve months to three years of age, a child's key developmental task is to successfully learn *autonomy*.[1]

> **autonomy** \ au 'taun oh me \ noun:
> Acting independently; a stage of self-directed freedom.

This is the stage where your preschooler recognizes he can act out his intentions, he has a voice, and—like the tree falling in the forest—he can be heard. There are *ripples* in the universe because of *him*.

Getting a Reaction Out of You

As an example, consider the "why?" response you get after you tell your preschooler something. When you answer that question, there comes another "why?" and then another "why?" It happens repeatedly. Why?

A young child asks why for two very different reasons. First, it's to gather information about this new world—one that's even bigger now that he can travel on his own. This world is full of excitement, newness, and interesting things. His brain is trying to collect as much sensory data as it can to build more and more connections.

Second, he's fascinated that what *he* does (asking why) has an impact on the *world* around him (you answer). Wow, that's amazing! (To your toddler or preschooler, that is.)

Similarly, your child will say no for the same reason. (*Golly gee ding dong,* can this word make ripples in the world!) What possesses little 36-pound Tyler to tell his 187-pound, six-foot-two father no when he's told it's time to get into bed? You and I know those are not good odds.

Remember, again, the tree-falling-in-the-forest question. Tyler simply has to verbalize this newly learned sound *no* and watch.

This huge man's face turns red.

His eyes bulge out.

And smoke comes out his ears!

Just imagine what's going on in a child's mind when the parent reacts to *no: You missed it? No problem. Watch, I'll do it again! "No." It's great, isn't it? I love this. Let me do it again. "No." I love this. I love this. I love—uh-oh. I think I'm in trouble!*

This is part of the magical thinking phase two-year-olds are in. They really do think they're not just the boss, but the king! *Look at all the power I have!* (Autonomy.) *I must be king! Wow! And I want to do that again, and again, and—*

And here's where the battle lines are drawn. Your toddler needs to learn experientially:

1. She does have control over her own behavior— verbally saying no or asking why.
2. The world changes by responding to what she initiates with her actions. Here we go with the subject of control. And control is a good thing here. It needs to be shaped, tempered, and used wisely because it *is* so powerful.
3. Power and control are shared. She does have *some*

power and control (not *all*), and so do you (not *all* either). And, by the way, your portion is larger than hers. You know that. I know that. She doesn't—yet.

Think of it as the swimming pool game, Marco-Polo, going on between parent and child. The child says, "Marco," and the world (you) responds, "Polo." He says, "Marco," again, and again the world (you) responds, "Polo." He is the tree falling in the forest (saying "Marco," or asking "why?" or saying "no," or repeating any other word that gets a reaction). And you, with your "Polo," or "Because," or "Yes, you will, young man," or however you respond, communicate:

- "I *did* hear you," which means,
- "You *do* exist," which helps your child conclude,
- *I do exist! Wow, I exist. And I have a voice, and wow, let's do that again!* "Why?"
- or "no,"—again and again and again.

Have you ever been through this "going-nowhere" conversation with your toddler or preschooler?

"Trevor, let me tuck you into bed. Do you want your covers on?"

"No."

"Do you want your covers off, then?"

"No."

"Do you want your covers hanging from the ceiling?"

"No."

"You don't want your covers at all, then?"

"No."

"So you want to sleep without your covers?"

"No."

"Good night, then!"

"Good night. Mommy, I love you."

Sound familiar?

Your interaction with your preschooler, regardless of what word he uses or how you respond, is introducing the necessary data into his little brain that he does, in fact, exist and he has a voice, too. Your response validates your preschooler because he is recognized at that moment in time.

This magical thinking phase means there *will be* challenges to your "boss-ship." That's the way it's experientially learned. It *has* to be challenged to become real. Realize that when your toddler challenges you, it's not because you're being a bad parent. It's part of the necessary learning process. Unfortunate, but true. It's okay. Not fun or pleasant, yet normal. So relax. There's no real pressure on you. It may be obvious to say, but remember that some personality types will challenge more than others.

Amen to that!

Initiative

During the next preschool developmental stage, from about three to six years of age, your child begins to understand his or her responsibility for those actions that cause a ripple in the universe. The developmental task facing your child now is learning to take initiative.[2]

> initiative \ a 'ni sha tive \ noun:
> The introductory, or first, action step.

Initiative is where "cause and effect" thinking begins forming. This sets the foundation for the responsibility struggles that are likely to come.

Helping your preschooler understand she has a choice is paramount to her healthy development. Yet newfound control and choice need to be tamed and trained to go in the proper direction. And this learning comes through trial and error—and there will be lots of "error" along the way. Errors are okay. Errors are part of the learning process. Errors can be great teachers—for your child as well as for you. Errors aren't necessarily fun, but they are manageable. Allowing for the existence of errors will take lots of pressure off your parenting.

Believe it or not, your child's autonomy/free will, your parental control, your child's initiative, your parental responsibility, the Three Rules of Life, and your influencing ability can blend comfortably and without added pressure on you.

"That sounds impossible to me. I'm all ears."

Relax, it really is easier than it looks. Let me explain.

Balancing Voice and Safety

Let's go back to the complicated task of choosing Sunday morning footwear.

1. As parents, we know snow is cold on the feet.
2. As parents, we expect the church parking lot to be plowed after a snowstorm.
3. As parents, we control the options available to Terryll. Notice that sandals are not one of the options.

4. As parents, we know whatever footwear Terryll chooses will not harm her.
5. As parents, we influence her choice with the side comment "Yay, snow boots!"
6. As parents, we put the choice in front of her—even before she asks. We are encouraging her to exercise her voice, her free will (*validate* and *nurture*).
7. As parents, we really don't care which she chooses. We don't take it personally, either, if she changes her mind (voice) right before getting into the car.
8. Terryll chooses—she exercises her voice—what she wants at the time.
9. As parents, we hear her voice and respond to her choice. (The tree falls in the forest and we are there to hear it, so she really does exist.)
10. If she chooses the snow boots, we praise her for her smart choice. We are showing her what sorts of things are on the smart list.
11. If she chooses the tennis shoes—well, her feet get a bit cold. We connect her choice to wear the tennis shoes with her cold feet (even though that's a bit abstract for a concrete-thinking preschooler) and suggest (teachable moment) she choose the snow boots next Sunday. We are showing her what sorts of things are on the stupid list.
12. If needed, we will warm her toes with our hands (*nurture*).
13. In the end, we get to church. Then we get home later and all is well.
14. Next Sunday we will have this conversation again.

"But *what if* your car slid off the road and into a snow bank, and *what if* you had to walk to safety? The tennis shoes would be the *wrong* footwear to have on. *Shouldn't* you have thought that through and *made* her wear boots?"

Are you hearing the stress traps? They're everywhere.

We didn't slide into a snow bank. And even if we had, we kept blankets, sleeping bags, a shovel, and emergency items in the car (our control). I would have carried her on my back so her feet wouldn't be in the snow in the first place (my control). We would be responsible parents. And all would be well.

The Sandal Scenario

"What would you do if Terryll wanted to wear sandals?"

Good question. Let's pick up the interaction at step eight:

8. Terryll says, "But I want to wear sandals!"

9. As parents, we say something like, "Do you *reeeeeally* want to wear sandals in all that cold and snow? *Brrr!* Your toes are going to get "owie" cold! Snow boots (yay, snow boots!) or your tennis shoes would be a smart choice." (We are *influencing* with our tone of voice.)

As parents, we allow our daughter to voice her opinion and make her request. We hear her and respond to her (again, the tree-falling-in-the-forest concept) and do not attempt to shut her down. We also redirect her to the original choice we placed in front of her. In doing so, we can use this as a teachable moment to highlight the difference between the smart list and the stupid list.

NOTE: Conversations like this may continue for some time, and they make excellent teachable moments. It's not a "her versus us" challenge.

10. We can redirect her to the original option with a statement like: "In the summer, sandals would be a great choice to make. But it's really cold out now, so that's why sandals aren't one of the choices for today. Your snow boots would be a *lot* better for your toes." (We are *influencing* with our tone of voice.)

11. If she chooses the snow boots, even if reluctantly with a bit of a push from us, we praise her for her smart choice. We are showing her what sorts of things are on the smart list.

12. If she chooses the tennis shoes, even if reluctantly with a bit of a push from us, we praise her for co-operating with the choices presented to her. Later, if her feet get cold, we warm her feet (*nurture*). Then we connect her choice to wear the tennis shoes with her cold feet (even though that's a bit abstract for a concrete-thinking preschooler) and suggest (teachable moment) she choose the snow boots next Sunday. We are showing her what sorts of things are on the stupid list yet again.

13. We go to church. Then we get home later and all is well.

Sandal Scenario Two

"But what would you do if Terryll kept insisting on wearing her sandals?"

Okay, let's pick up the interaction again at step eight:

8. Terryll insists, "But I want to wear my sandals!"
9. The response: "Terryll, there are only two choices for today." In a lower, slower tone of voice: "So do you want to wear your snow boots or your tennis shoes?"
10. "But I want to wear my sandals!"
11. "We heard you. Not today. It's time to choose *either* your snow boots or your tennis shoes. Which will it be?"
12. "But, I—"
13. "Terryll," (saying a person's name often causes that person's brain to slow down and hear you better— which is exactly what we want) "choose either your snow boots or your tennis shoes, or we will choose your snow boots for you."
14. If she chooses the snow boots, even if reluctantly with a bit of a push from us, we praise her for the smart choice she made. We are showing her what sorts of things are on the smart list.
15. If she chooses the tennis shoes, even if reluctantly with a bit of a push from us, we praise her for cooperating with the choices presented to her. If her feet get cold, we warm them (*nurture*). We connect her choice to wear the tennis shoes with her cold feet and suggest she choose the snow boots next Sunday.

16. If she doesn't choose, we follow up with "You just made a choice not to choose, so we're choosing your snow boots for you so your toes will stay warm and cozy."
17. We then proceed to put snow boots on her feet.
18. "Noooooo! I want my tennis shoes!"

Check yourself here. It's important to stick to the original issue—her choice of what to wear to church. Don't turn this into a "because I said so" issue or get off track with her choosing tennis shoes after you chose the snow boots. Stay with the real issue at hand. Otherwise your child will get confused and not understand what is being taught and what to learn.

Question: Did Terryll *choose* either her snow boots or her tennis shoes?

She *did* choose (her voice, her control) one of the options we offered her (our control). The issue was validating and encouraging her choice, directing her free-will voice to choose the smart list, and rewarding her for her choice to cooperate and obey (which she did because she chose from within the parameters we set for her).

What creates many parent/child tensions is when we (parents) turn a simple issue of choosing shoes to wear to church into a complicated issue of obedience, submission, respect, and so on. It becomes about us and our parenting, rather than the simple issue of choosing shoes. The shoe issue turns into a *make sure they turn out right* or *make sure I do everything right* issue, intentionally or not. That's exactly where the stress and pressure come from.

Low-pressure parenting says:

It's shoes.

It's getting to church.

It's keeping her toes safe some way or another.

That's all.

Relax, mission accomplished. Good parenting.

19. And if her final choice was tennis shoes, it's just like step fifteen. Nurture her by warming her feet, teach her about tennis shoes in cold weather, and suggest she try the snow boots next time.

20. We would go to church. We would get home later and all would be well.

Sandal Scenario Three

Depending on the specific situation, we could also take the dialogue in the following direction.

8. Terryll says, "But I want to wear sandals!"

9. As parents, we could say, "Terryll, wearing your sandals when it's cold and snowy outside is a foolish choice. It would be smart to choose your snow boots or your tennis shoes."

10. "But I want to wear my sandals!"

11. "We heard you. So even though it's a foolish choice to wear sandals rather than snow boots (yay, snow boots!), we will allow you (because we're still in control, we're the ones who allowed sandals to become a choice) to

'wear your sandals this time. No more discussion; let's get your sandals on and get in the car."

"Wait! Hold it! Didn't you just give in to your child? You just let her boss you around! Your authority was undermined. *Shouldn't* you have forced the issue?"

No. Consider the rest of the scenario.

12. As parents, we know her toes will get cold in her sandals.
13. As parents, we secretly slip socks and snow boots into the car.

Notice, we don't include both her boots and her tennis shoes. She made her choice already. Now it's the snow boots. We are in control of the situation and wouldn't allow any harm to come to her toes. At the same time, we allow Terryll the opportunity to experience the consequence of her foolish choice (Rule Three).

14. Off to church we go.
15. And as parents, if need be, we are ready to rescue our daughter from her own foolish choice and make sure she—and her toes—will be fine (*nurture*).
16. We get to church. We go home later and all is well.

So are we still responsible parents in the preceding scenario?

Did we allow Terryll to voice and exercise her free will? Yes.

And did we cooperate with the Three Rules of Life? Yes.

Did we still make sure our daughter—and her toes—were safe?

"I guess so. But *I* wouldn't do it that way," the skeptic in you might say.

That's fine. Remember, though, we're dealing with life in the third circle out—the *general guidelines*. So we're not doing anything wrong or foolish; it's just different from what you would do.

It Will Work

This is how all those pieces flow together in a low-pressure way. It's your child's voice and autonomy. It's your control and influence as the parent. This is not an *either/or* but, rather, a *both/and* dynamic. There's no need to unconsciously fight an *either/or* battle. Take the pressure off yourself. Give your child a voice. *Validate* that voice. *Nurture* that voice. Praise him for what he did correctly. As for the parts he missed, show him a smart way of doing it next time in words he can understand.

In the book *Outliers*, Malcolm Gladwell repeatedly mentions what's called the "10,000-hour rule."[3] According to this rule, it takes 10,000 hours of deliberate practice to gain a sense of mastery of a skill. To truly master that skill, you will need more than just that many hours of deliberate practice.

Mastering a skill is most easily seen and understood in the world of sports. For your daughter to be an elite gymnast and reach her peak performance by the time she's twelve to fifteen years old, she will need to begin tumbling classes when she's three years old. If you want your son to make the club soccer advanced leagues that will set him up for World Cup play in his twenties, he will need to start chasing a soccer ball around before he enters kindergarten. Like it or not, that's how long—how many hours of purposeful practice—it will take for your daughter or son to master a sport in time to make the "big leagues," as we say.

When it comes to such critical life skills as learning cause-and-effect thinking, accepting delayed gratification, establishing a solid work ethic, or learning to think critically and wisely, the necessary years of "practice" don't seem as obvious. But these life skills are much more important to master than a sport or a musical instrument. If you want your child to master these and other life skills, begin now. Link his (instant) choice to eat his cookie now with not getting a cookie later when the rest of the family enjoys theirs (delayed). Link her obedience to you and getting ready for bed without a fuss with the reward of story time or the back rub she can enjoy once snug in bed. Link his help with taking out the trash to a sense of accomplishment and healthy pride.

Mastering life skills is more than a collection of learned behaviors like tying his shoes or learning her ABCs. Learned behaviors come fairly quickly with a few months of repetition. Mastering life skills, on the other hand, takes about 10,000 hours of purposeful practice.

So link, link, and link some more. And begin now.

Your preschooler will need many hours of practicing her skills in using her autonomous voice and taking initiative. If you want your son or daughter to be skilled in making wise choices when it comes to what shoes to wear in the Colorado winter when she's a teenager, when will you begin giving her opportunities to practice such choices and learn what's on the smart and stupid lists? You can't wait until she's a teenager. You need to—for her sake—begin when she's a toddler. That's why you give your toddler controlled choices and let him or her make the choice.

Here's a great interchange to use with your preschooler. After taking the time to explain something to him, ask, "Get it?" and teach him to respond with "Got it!" (when he actually does get it). That's teaching him autonomy and initiative.

This will make more sense when we look at what I call the Grid in chapter 7.

STEP AWAY FROM
THE POWER STRUGGLE

SEVEN

GOOD NEWS! YOU'RE NOT IN CONTROL

It's TRUE THAT contemporary culture puts added stress and pressure on you as a parent. It's true your preschooler holds the "wild card" called free will.

But (and this is a very important *but*) parenting is *still* a doable job. Remember, you simply need to know what you *can* control and what you *can't* control.

Easy, right?

Not necessarily easy, but still doable.

That reassurance can feel hard to grasp when your daughter has just lied to your face for the fourth time in one day. Or when your son manages to spread kitty litter all over the garage—and promises it wasn't his fault.

This chapter will provide you with practical tools you can

use to make smart and healthy moves when parenting. To use these tools, you'll want to have a clear understanding of the terms *control, influence,* and *responsibility.*

Here we go.

control \ kon 'troll \ verb:
   To have direct and complete power over; to be the only variable in the outcome of a situation.

Control or Not

When it comes to raising children, and pretty much everything else in life, all of life really can be divided up into two major categories: what you *can* control and what you *can't* control.

WHAT **I CAN** **CONTROL**	**WHAT** **I CAN'T** **CONTROL**

Given this definition of control, what legitimately fits into the category of what you can control? Give this question real thought before you continue reading. What do you *really* have control over?

Hint: The answer is not "nothing."

What legitimately fits into the category of "what I can control"? There are only three things: me, myself, and I. That's it. Before getting discouraged, be reassured there is *always* something, some piece of any given circumstance you do have control over. It may not include as much control as you'd like. It may not include control over the people you'd like. While you can't control the specific situation, you *can* control your response to the particular situation and your attitude toward it.

It may be only the opportunity to choose between a rock and a hard place, but there is always something you *can* control. Even if you have only a shred of control—even if it's a hard shred to find—you do have some control. There is *always* a choice you can make.

Since that's all that fits into the "what I can control" category, guess what fits into the "what I can't control" category?

*Every*thing and *every*body else.

That's a whole lot of the world. That's more than seven billion human beings, not to mention pets, natural elements, and events. As a parent, you do have a lot of *influencing* power (and our look at that is coming later in the book). Right now we're on the subject of *control* because one thing that makes parenting less stressful is understanding—and accepting—this part of life.

Do you like the way the world is divided up where control is concerned? Most people don't. They aren't looking to control the *whole* world, but most would like *more* control, especially over things that have a direct impact on their children.

That's not reality.

You control what *you* do: all your actions and behaviors.

You control what *you* think and believe: your values, attitudes, and opinions.

You control how *you* express and manage your emotions.

But you can't control the weather.

You can't control every part of any given circumstance.

You can't control the future, which doesn't even exist at this time and place.

You can't control other people. This includes your preschooler.

You just can't.

But you *do* have a lot of control over your child's environment, the options you present to her, and the circumstances you place her in.

Remember our family "fourteener" outing?

I controlled which fourteener we were going to climb.

I watched the weather and controlled whether we kept climbing or turned back as a family.

I controlled making sure I had extra gear for each of the girls, just in case.

I controlled holding on to Heidi to keep her from being blown off the ridge.

All these things fit into the "I control what I *do*" category of life. I also had control over how and when I used my *influencing* power during that day. As parents, we do have control—just not over our kids.

You control who babysits your child.

You control when and if your son has a play date at his friend's house.

You control which options you set before your daughter when it comes to picking Sunday footwear.

You control whether you let your friend's daughter—who might have the chicken pox—come over to your home.

And yes, *you* control if Grandma takes your preschooler for an overnight stay. It may not be easy, but it's still your decision because you are the parent.

You control numerous aspects of the environment around your preschooler—just not your preschooler. (Repetition is good for learning, even with parents.)

Got it? Does that sound better?

Hope so.

Trying to control what you can't equals HIGH pressure when it comes to parenting.

Accepting the truth that you can't control all you'd like, and focusing on how to best influence, equals LOW-pressure parenting.

Besides, it's not your job to *make them turn out right*. You can't control the outcome. So stop trying.

"So if my twenty-two-month-old chooses to stick a paper clip into an electrical outlet, it's not my fault? I mean, I didn't choose the foolish behavior—he did—so it's not my fault, right?"

Right. It's not your fault your son chose to stick a paper clip into the electrical outlet. However, what *is* your fault was choosing to leave an outlet unprotected. That *is* your responsibility. That was *your* choosing. So *that is* your fault.

Clearer now?

Responsible or Not

We'll divide the same world we live in into two other categories: what you *are* responsible for and what you're *not* responsible for.

```
┌─────────────────────────────┐
│                             │
│            WHAT             │
│          I TAKE             │
│       RESPONSIBILITY        │
│            FOR              │
│                             │
├─────────────────────────────┤
│                             │
│            WHAT             │
│        I DON'T TAKE         │
│       RESPONSIBILITY        │
│            FOR              │
│                             │
└─────────────────────────────┘
```

responsible \ re 'spon sa 'bull \ adjective:
Able to respond. (The only things you can legitimately respond to are the things you have control over.)

Being responsible means taking legitimate ownership of what is mine to be in charge of—in control of—in appropriate ways, and doing whatever needs to be done. I have a 2008 Jeep. It's mine. I own it. I also take *responsibility* for it. How? I pay the registration fee. I put gas in the tank. I see that it gets the proper maintenance. I wash it. I do whatever is appropriate to do for my Jeep. I'm acting responsibly. And in doing so, I reap the benefits of having an awesome vehicle.

I'm *not* responsible for *your* vehicle. Why not? Because it's not mine. I don't own it. I'm not in a position to "respond" to it. Your vehicle belongs to you. And if it belongs to you, you control it. You're responsible for it, not me. It's not that I don't like your vehicle. It's just not *my* vehicle. I don't control it. I can't control it. I'm not responsible for it. I'm just not, plain and simple.

Don't you sometimes—or often—feel pressure coming from other parents or adults to be "responsible" (somehow, some way) for your toddler's actions?

What will my in-laws think if I don't make (or force?) my son to give them hugs when they come to visit?

What will Marie think of me when she finds out my daughter threw a fit in the nursery this morning?

Care to add any of your own "What will they think if . . ." statements to the list? Such statements—real or perceived—can make you *feel* "responsible" for your child's actions and attitudes, even when you're actually *not* responsible. Sounds a whole lot like Stress Trap Two, doesn't it?

Now look at yourself for a moment. Have you ever evaluated another parent based on his or her preschooler's behavior? Have you ever thought another parent was "responsible" for his or her child's actions? Social pressure (with its *should* and *shouldn't* statements) can be a huge obstacle to healthy parenting and our sanity, heaping pressure and stress onto our shoulders. Be careful; don't fall for it. Don't do it either.

You can't *control* other people. So you can't be *responsible* for things you can't control. You may have to clean up the mess afterward, but the mess wasn't your fault. That's reality.

It's not your fault if your child chooses foolishly. It's only your fault if *you* choose foolishly as the parent.

"How does a parent mind his or her own business and still parent?"

To answer that question, look at the following diagram. I call it the Grid. (It's empty now, but it will fill up soon.)

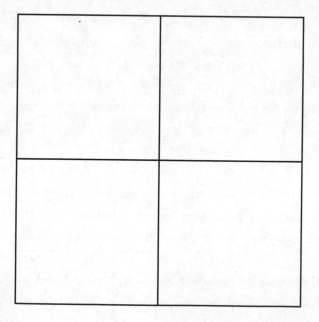

There are four boxes, or quadrants, in our diagram. Each quadrant represents a specific style of relating to or interacting with another person. These are not personality types (which are mostly unchangeable) but ways you and your preschooler may *interact relationally* in any given situation.

A person can use any one of the four styles. In fact, you may find yourself or your child bouncing back and forth among different styles during the same conversation about the same topic.

It will make more sense as we look at each style in more detail.

HOLD

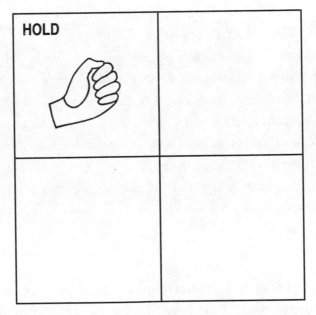

HOLD represents the interacting style that combines "what I *can* control" with "what I take responsibility for."

If you are a HOLDer, the following terms accurately describe you or your child:

- responsible
- honest; truthful with yourself and others
- trustworthy; others can count on you to follow through with what you control
- willing to accept consequences
- taking ownership of yourself

The HOLDer says, "What's mine is mine." When you use this interaction style, you hold on to the things that are legitimately yours to control and that you are responsible for. You're holding on to what is yours to own. You keep what's yours to keep. You're responsible for it.

Anybody relating in this way will have confidence. I'm not talking about self-esteem; I mean a confidence in one's abilities and character. *Confidence is in direct proportion to honesty.* If this is you, you're being honest with yourself and others.

We teach this relational style to our children so they will eventually interact in healthy ways with others. This is one of the two healthy styles of interacting, whether you're the preschooler or the parent.

TOSS

TOSS represents the interacting style that combines "what I *can* control" with "what I *don't* take responsibility for."

If you—or your preschooler—is a TOSSer, the following terms accurately describe you or your child:

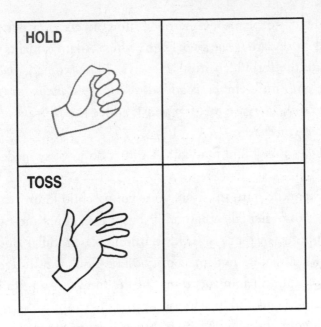

- irresponsible
- liar, denier, blamer; pointing fingers at everybody else for your own actions
- avoider: You avoid responding to what is legitimately yours
- untrustworthy
- shirking consequences any way you can

The TOSSer says, "What's mine is yours."

When you use this style, you toss off your responsibilities. You attempt to toss your stuff onto somebody else, for *him or her* to handle, fix, be responsible for, and bear the consequences of.

This interactive style is where toddlers and preschoolers naturally begin. As human beings, we all have the sinful tendency to blame. Remember the conversation between God and Adam (Genesis 3:12) in which Adam explains why he ate the forbidden fruit? He says, "The woman *you* put here with me" (emphasis added—*tossing the blame in God's direction*), "*she* gave me" (emphasis added—*tossing the blame in Eve's direction*).

Does this sound familiar? "I didn't do it. Sissy made me do it."

From the start, this is all your young child knows to do. It's in his or her fallen nature, just as it is in yours and mine. It's normal in that sense. It's natural. Your toddler doesn't know yet that it's not smart or good or God's way. It doesn't help to punish him for doing all he knows to do. Rather, teach him and lead him in the way of the truth. As a parent, teach your child God's way of being responsible for what is his or hers. Model the way to become a HOLDer.

If you think only preschoolers are capable of TOSSing, blaming, and unloading, think again.

The TOSSer says: "Son, *you* made me late for work today." "Can't you see *you're* making your mother cry? She can't help worrying about you." "If *you'd* stop misbehaving, maybe we could have some sanity in this house again."

It's easy for parents to be TOSSers as well.

Since *confidence grows in direct proportion to honesty*, and people using the TOSS style are not being honest, this interaction style will erode confidence. Even if I get away with blaming somebody else, and he or she takes the consequences for my actions, I still won't gain genuine confidence.

This is *not* a healthy style of interaction to use. It won't help anybody.

GRAB

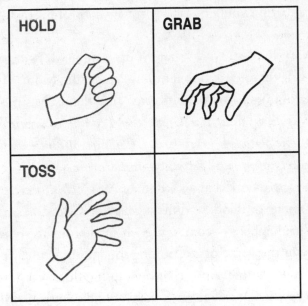

GRAB represents the interacting style that combines "what I *can't* control" with "what I take responsibility for."

For a GRABer, the following descriptions often would be accurate:

- over responsible; trying to bear burdens that aren't legitimately yours
- fixer, rescuer, enabler, codependent
- martyr; an "Oh, poor me" person
- accepting consequences for wrongs you didn't even commit
- overcontrolling or intimidating
- control freak
- thinking problems are your fault: "If only I would—"

- manipulator; trying to force the outcome of a situation you have no legitimate control over

The GRABer says, "What's yours is mine." It's all too easy to re-title this box "Conscientious Parent" or "Mom." This is a style of interacting parents often find themselves in. They think, *If it's my fault as a parent, then I can fix it, because I'm a responsible person. If I can fix it, it will turn out the way I want it to. And nobody will get hurt—including me.*

It doesn't work that way. Remember God's gift called free will? You're not God, so don't try playing God.

What happens to confidence when you use this style? You can't win the game of controlling something you can't control. So you'll lose. And what does losing do to confidence? It destroys it. Or if it appears that you did win, you will gain a *false sense* of confidence. Either way, it's not a healthy relating style—no matter how spiritual we make it sound. It's not healthy to take responsibility for things you can't control— nor is it based on truth.

FOLD

FOLD represents the interacting style that combines "what I *can't* control" with "what I *don't* take responsibility for."

Think of FOLDing your hands in front of you. If you're a FOLDer, the following words could be used to describe you:

- simply *not* responsible
- honest; letting others know what's yours and what's theirs

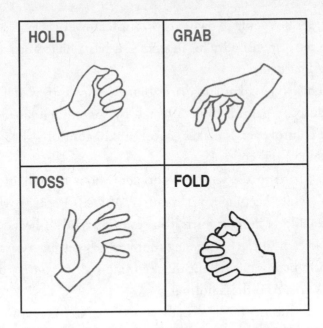

- trustworthy; you keep your hands off what doesn't belong to you
- allowing consequences to fall where they belong, even when it's hard to stand by and watch
- not taking ownership of the other person's stuff

FOLDers say, "What's yours is yours." This is the other healthy style of interaction.

Using this style of relating may give the *appearance* that you don't care, but that's not true. For example, "I do care about your car; it's just not my vehicle to wash."

We're affected daily by things we have no control over. It's easy to fall into the trap of thinking, *Well, since it affects me, I should have some control over it!* In doing so, you slide up the diagram and end up interacting as a GRABer.

If it's not yours to own, keep your hands FOLDed. Don't take the responsibility for it, even if it has a huge impact on you. That's life.

This style is harder to use than it may appear at first. Because it's painful to be affected by something you don't have control over. It makes us feel "out of control"—because it *is* out of our control.

It's hard to see your preschooler "shoot himself in the foot" while keeping your hands FOLDed. Because when your child is hurt, it hurts you, too. It's hard to hear your son scream in the emergency room as he's getting a cast on his arm because he fell off the retaining wall in your yard. It just hurts. And that's normal.

Still, the truth is, "What's yours is yours" and "What's theirs is theirs."

HOLD and FOLD

Remember to HOLD and FOLD—the healthy styles of interacting. Keep away from the TOSS and GRAB styles. Those are the unhealthy ways of interacting with others— especially your preschooler.

If you are already HOLDing and FOLDing, great! Keep up the good work. Stand your ground; you're doing it right.

As parents we're left taking our wounded, broken, tired, and scared hearts to God over and over again. You signed up to have your heart broken when you became a parent. You didn't know that? It was written in small print inside the wristband your baby wore home from the hospital.

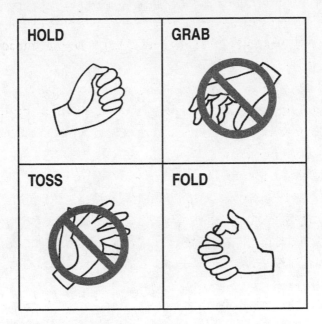

"But I never saw this coming."

No, you didn't. And it still hurts.

You do, however, have a useful tool that will help you parent in the tough times. That tool is *influence*. Turn the page and we'll see how to use it wisely and well.

EIGHT

INFLUENCE: A HEALTHY WAY
TO DANCE

Now FOR THE moment you've been waiting for. What is *influence*, and what does it look like?

influence \ 'in flu ents \ noun:
The act of producing an effect without using force; swaying, inspiring, impressing, or moving something. Being only one of several variables to the outcome.

Influence can be overt or covert, subtle or blatant, mild or wild. As a parent, you have a powerful presence in your child's life, and that grants you tremendous influence. Exercising that power wisely is part of your responsibility as a parent. Keeping the power to influence while letting go of the control you really don't have in the first place is easier when you understand the difference between the two. It is—like all these parts of parenting—doable. And doing so keeps the pressure low.

What separates influence from control is that in all your powerful persuading and inspiring (1) you don't force, and (2) you still allow the other person to make the final choice. Your preschooler still keeps the control over her free will. She is still responsible for her personal actions, thoughts, and feelings. Yes, you encourage her to see things your way. Yes, you try to talk her out of doing something irresponsible she's thinking of doing. Yet with all those powerful attempts to inspire, sway, motivate, and infiltrate your daughter's thought process—which parents need never feel ashamed of—you still don't force her thinking or behavior by coercing or manipulating. You let her choose and retain the control that is rightfully hers. It's as much a matter of motive as it is behavior.

Note: I'm talking about circumstances that won't cause your child the damaging kind of pain (see "The Two Kinds of Pain" in chapter 5 if you need that reminder).

Here's another way to look at the difference between control and influence:

Control exists when you are the *only* variable to the outcome of the situation.

Influence exists when you are *one of several* variables to the outcome of the situation.

"So, if I *make* my daughter wear her snow boots, am I trying to control her or influence her?"

That's a great question, and the answer is found not in the "snow boots or tennis shoes" choice, but rather in your motive—the relational "dance" you're doing with your daughter.

Dances with Preschoolers

Based on the Grid—the four styles of interaction described in chapter 7—four possible dances can unfold any time two people interact. This is true whenever two human beings interact at work, at church, in the community, in the grocery store, at a family reunion, or in your kitchen. Any place and any time two humans interact, you'll find one of these dances taking place, even between parent and child.

Let's consider true-to-life examples of a parent interacting with a preschooler. As you read the following scenarios, see how they relate to your own relationship patterns with your child.

Dance One: The HOLD and GRAB

In this dance, the preschooler uses the HOLD style of relating. In spite of limited maturity and relational ability, this child is doing his very best to HOLD on to control. His position is "What's mine is mine."

The parent attempts to GRAB control: "What's yours is mine."

This dance is rare, but it still occurs from time to time. Let's see how it unfolds in the following parent-child scene. (I'll play the part of the four-year-old son, Tim.)

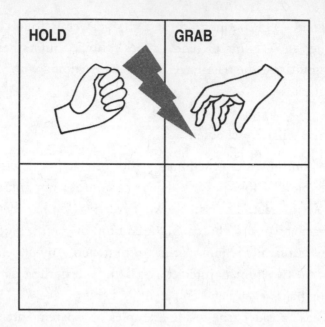

HOLD	GRAB

MOM: "Tim, did you take the marker off my desk and write all over your face?"

TIM: "Ummm, yes."

(I'm HOLDing. I'm attempting to take ownership of my marked-up face.)

MOM: "Honey, I'm so sorry I left my black marker out. I guess I *should* have remembered to put it away. I didn't even think about it. Let's go wash your face, and that will make things all better."

(Notice that Mom never addressed the fact that I took something off her desk without asking. She's GRABing. Her motive is to take the ownership and blame for my choice to write all over my face. It's not the same as validating my feelings and helping me take the ownership for myself. She's trying to fix something that's not hers to fix.)

TIM: "I'm sorry I took it off your desk."

(I'm still HOLDing. Remember, this is rare.)

MOM: "No, I'm sorry I haven't been paying much attention lately. It's my fault."

(She's still GRABing.)

TIM: "Umm, but you said never—"

MOM: "No 'buts.' And don't argue with me."

Believe it or not, this dance actually happens from time to time. We don't see it easily because often the preschooler's attempt to take ownership of his or her actions may not be complete or effective.

This dance always produces tension, strain, and pressure. Why? Because both participants are trying to own the same thing; both are attempting to take control of the marked-up face. Two objects cannot occupy the same space at the same time. That's simple physics. Two human beings cannot own the same thing at the same time. That's simple human relations.

But wait! Who's using the healthy style of interacting? The preschooler. The tension isn't the child's fault because he's trying to control what's his. He's trying to do the responsible thing, though his attempt may not appear that way to his mother.

Who's using an unhealthy style of interacting? The parent. She needs to make the move. As the child tries to HOLD on to control, the parent GRABs the control away. The child may not even realize it, but the parent is trying to take away his free will.

Mom needs to take her hands off and let her child learn from his own choices. We'll delve more deeply into this when we get to Dance Four.

In place of Dance One—or after it's gone on for a while—what often happens is this: In order to eliminate the tension and obey the parent, the child moves to Dance Two. Let's see how that dialogue might go.

Dance Two: The TOSS and GRAB

In this dance, the preschooler uses the TOSS style of interaction: "What's mine is yours."

The parent is still using the GRAB style, trying to hold on to control: "What's yours is mine."

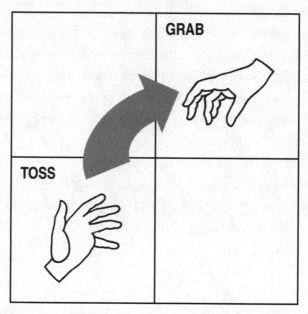

MOM: "Tim, did you take the marker off my desk and write all over your face?"

TIM: "No."

(I'm TOSSing. I'm attempting to deny or push the ownership of my marked-up face away.)

MOM: "Honey, I'm so sorry I left my black marker out. I guess I *should* have remembered to put it away. Let's go wash your face, and that will make things all better."

(Mom's GRABing, as in the previous example.)

TIM (thinking): *Okay, great! I'm not in trouble after all.* End of discussion.

Does this dance sound familiar to you? It's far more common than Dance One in a house with a preschooler. The terrible thing about this dance is that it works. There's no real tension here. It's like the game of "throw and catch." The preschooler TOSSes—and the parent GRABs.

The problem with this dance is the TOSSing goes in only one direction—away from the child and toward the parent. This doesn't mean all is well and healthy in your kitchen. It's not. But at least the tension and fighting between parent and child won't continue. These two unhealthy styles of interacting do work together, though not in a healthy way.

Often the diffusion of tension accomplished by the TOSS and GRAB dance gives a sense to both parent and child that all is well and the parent is acting responsibly. It's also a great way for a preschooler to gain a false sense of power and for a parent to gain a false sense of being needed.

Dance Three: The TOSS and FOLD

In this style of interaction, the child is still TOSSing: "What's mine is yours."

The parent, however, uses the FOLD style of interaction: "What's yours is yours." Let's consider our sample dialogue when this dynamic is at work.

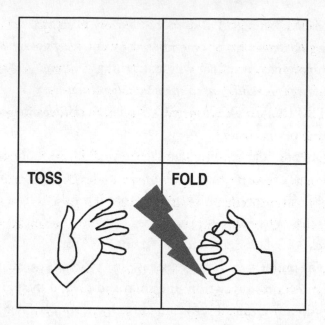

MOM: "Tim, did you take the marker off my desk and write all over your face?"

TIM: "No."

(I'm TOSSing.)

MOM: "Honey, I see you have marker marks all over your face. I'm so sorry I left my black marker out. You know not to take things off Mommy's desk without asking first. That was a foolish choice *you* made."

(Notice that Mom responded with almost the same words as she did in the TOSS and GRAB dance. Almost. So what makes this dance different? See how the pronoun you *is emphasized. It makes all the difference in the world.)*

MOM: "Let's go wash your face, and then you'll sit at the dining room table for a five-minute time-out, and that will make things all better."

(Mom's hands are FOLDed. She's not accepting this. She's not taking the responsibility or the blame for her child's marked-up face or disobedience. She's not GRABing for control. She's trying to influence her child, yes, but not control the outcome.)

TIM: "But it wasn't *my* fault. You even said *you* forgot to put the marker away!"

MOM: "No, Tim. It's *not* my fault. I did leave the marker out on my desk. It was still *your choice* to disobey and take the marker off my desk and mark all over your face."

TIM: "But *you* didn't put it away. You even said so yourself."

(The child tries to TOSS the blame on Mom again, but there's no control or power struggle here. Mom is refusing to GRAB, and in doing so she's influencing her child to HOLD the consequences of his own foolish choice.)

MOM: "No, Tim. It's *not* my fault. It was still *your* choice to disobey and take the marker off my desk and mark all over your face. I still love you."

If, or when, you're caught up in this dance with one of your children and you're FOLDing, hold your ground! You're exercising the correct interaction style. You're doing it right. Yes, there's tension, but that's not your fault. The tension is because someone—in this case, your preschooler—is using an unhealthy style of interacting, and you're not letting him get away with it. Sure, it can be tiring, but if you keep holding your ground, one of two things will happen:

1. The tension will continue. That's a bummer, but don't cave in.

2. Your child will eventually make the move up the Grid and start being a HOLDer. Good for you! That's why you keep standing your ground—because it will *influence* your preschooler to make better choices.

"How long do I let the discussion go on? I mean, my preschooler could argue all day long, and I don't have all day."

That's an important question. My wife used to tell our daughters that she would keep talking and listening *as long as* (1) there was legitimate time to do so, and (2) as long as the conversation remained a discussion. Young children don't have a good understanding of time because it's an abstract concept they can't wrap their minds around. So if the available time is ending, tell your child the conversation is over for now and can be rescheduled for a later, specific time.

discussion \ dis 'ka shon \ noun:
When two people talk *and* listen to each other.
When the end goal is to sort the matter out.

argument \ 'ar guu ment \ noun:
When two people talk but *don't* listen to each
other. When the end goal is to get the other person
to agree to your point.

If the discussion becomes an argument, the interchange is over. This is another great teachable moment about the difference between the smart list and the stupid list. It won't diffuse the tension because the dance is still going. It does, however, stop the arguing and chaos. Easier said than done, I know.

The desired outcome is for your child to become a HOLDer. And the more you FOLD, the better the chances that this growth—from TOSSer to HOLDer—will take root in your child. As that happens, the dance becomes less frequent and usually shorter even if it does begin. That's an improvement!

If you give in and GRAB just to relieve the tension, you've gone back to the TOSS and GRAB dance. Don't do that. Stand your ground. There's a lot at stake.

An interesting study on the emotional stability level of college students across the country reports that, in general, college students can't handle normal struggles and problems of life.[1] These students interpret normal problems, dilemmas, and failures as end-of-the-world catastrophes, so they end up in counseling for anxiety or depression—some to the point of being suicidal. Remember the TOSS and FOLD dance as we consider outcomes for students in this study:

1. Students have an increased tendency to see poor grades as a reason to complain rather than as a reason to study more or more effectively. *(They are TOSSing.)*
2. Students are afraid to fail, so they don't take risks.
3. Students are very uncomfortable in not being right.
4. Students want "do-overs" (in college) if they didn't get the grades they want, rather than accepting the grades they earned. *(This is another form of TOSSing.)*
5. Students weren't given the opportunity to learn how to solve their own problems because the parents solved their problems for them. *(The parents GRABed.)*

6. Students didn't have the opportunity to get into trouble and find their own way out, to experience failure and realize they could survive it. *(See the Three Rules of Life.)*

7. Students are still unable or unwilling to take responsibility for themselves, feeling that if a problem arises, they need someone else to solve it for them. (*TOSS.*)

As hard as it may be for you to FOLD when your preschooler TOSSes, stand firm. Yes, it's a pain, but you're doing exactly what your preschooler needs you to do. You're *influencing* even when it's difficult for you. Influencing will pay off when this preschooler of yours finally starts college and/or enters adult life some day.

Dance Four: The HOLD and FOLD

In this interaction, the preschooler is HOLDing, taking responsibility for what he can control: "What's mine is mine."

The parent is a FOLDer. He or she doesn't take responsibility for what can't be controlled: "What's yours is yours."

MOM: "Tim, did you take the marker off Mommy's desk and write all over your face?"

TIM: "Yes."

(I'm HOLDing. I'm owning the problem.)

MOM: "Honey, I'm so sorry I left my black marker out. I'm really proud of you for making the smart choice to tell me the truth. You know not to take things off the desk

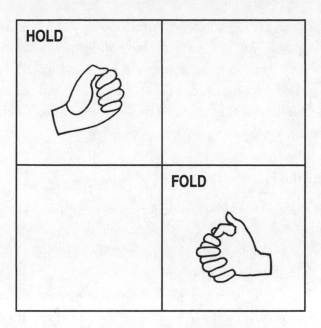

without asking first. You made a foolish choice. Let's go wash your face, and then you will sit at the dining room table for a five-minute time-out, and that will make things all better."

(Mom is FOLDing, letting me accept the consequences of my behavior. She is trying to influence me, yes, but not control the outcome.)

TIM: "Do I have to?"

MOM: "Yes, you do. It might help you remember to make a smart choice the next time and ask Mommy first."

(Mom is offering some good advice—"Ask first"—as a way to influence me. And she's sticking to her guns.)

TIM: "Okay."

MOM: "I still love you."

When you find this dance unfolding in your kitchen, and you're the FOLDer, you're doing it correctly. Yes, it's a lot easier to FOLD when your preschooler wisely decides to HOLD. Still, you get the credit for doing the right thing—FOLDing. Even when he attempts to HOLD, but isn't doing a very good job of it—still FOLD. Come alongside him and model how to HOLD more wisely. Remember, don't slide up the control grid and GRAB. Stay your course.

Doing the Healthy Dance

Which of the four possible dances is most common in your kitchen?

What about your family members? Which styles of interaction do they use most often?

Which style do you end up using most often?

Remember, if there's tension in the relationship with your preschooler, someone is most likely not using a healthy interaction style. Be sure it's not you. If it is, read, journal, or talk with a friend, pastor, or counselor. Do whatever works in order to get yourself out of the TOSS or GRAB style. It's not good for you, your preschooler, or the other family members.

If you regularly HOLD and FOLD, good work. Keep it up and keep leading by your example. It's doable, even in the face of tension and turmoil.

Low-Pressure Principle 4

. . . .

REDUCE THE RULES

NINE

CREATING ORDER WITHOUT ORDERING EVERYONE AROUND

- No checking your brother's diapers.
- No drinking from another kid's sippy cup.
- Bow your head and close your eyes whenever somebody prays.
- No eating the cat's food.

These are real household rules from families in real homes. Do any of these rules—or others like them—exist in your house? Think about your family's rules and try to remember what caused you to create them. Often a rule lives on long after its initial purpose is forgotten—especially with a preschooler's short attention span.

A conversation about rules can resemble trying to change

a dirty diaper in an airplane restroom: It's awkward and full of surprises, not all of them pleasant. The subject of rules is complicated by the fact that rules are often made in reaction to specific, unpleasant events. In the heat of the moment, parents step in and decree a new rule so "it won't happen again."

Making spur-of-the-moment rules can cause several problems. First, suddenly reacting to a bad situation can leave a parent feeling out of control. The rule established may not even be practical, but now everyone in the family has to live with it.

Second, we may attempt to use rules to control our preschooler's behavior. But rules *can't* control anybody's behavior—present or future. Remember, it's pointless to try to control something we can't—a preschooler's outward behavior, developing belief system, or attitude. If you're attempting to control a preschooler's behavior, there's a good possibility you have some *what-ifs* looming close by (Stress Trap Two). This worry thinking also results in that out-of-control feeling.

Third, as parents we sometimes decree rules in an attempt to keep our own worries in check. It's common for a parent to think something like *If Hanna never uses a fork, then I won't have to worry about her stabbing herself or her younger brother.*

That's a little exaggerated, but you get the point.

If your thinking rolls along these lines, please revisit chapter 4. The issue of worry is your problem, not your child's problem. You need to deal with it, not make your child suffer because of your anxiety.

The Reasons for Rules

There will *always* be rules. That's life. There will never be a place with no rules whatsoever. For some reason, humankind has come to believe in—and hope for—a place where there are no rules. It's not going to exist. Your workplace has rules. Whenever you get into your automobile to drive to the mall, you follow rules. School has rules. The grocery store has rules. All sports activities have rules. Even heaven and hell will have rules, I suppose. Call me old-fashioned, but I support the idea of "your house; your rules." That's life too.

Let's consider the Garden of Eden again. In this perfect place with perfect children and a perfect Parent, there was a rule: "Do not eat of that tree." It was a simple, clear command right in the center circle of the target we talked about in chapter 5.

Why was there a rule in the Garden? The answer lies in the two reasons for any rule:

1. To keep safety in
2. To keep chaos ("un-safety") out

That's as complicated as it gets. That's it.

Since you probably don't have a dictionary with you, let me review what *safety* and *chaos* mean.

safety \ 'saaf tee \ noun:
Being protected from physical, emotional, and/or spiritual damage or danger.

It's important to further clarify what safety means here. Remember "The Two Kinds of Pain" in chapter 5? When we talk about safety, we're talking about the second kind of pain that actually causes damage or destruction. The first kind of pain hurts—that's why it's called *pain*—but it's not doing any *damage*. It's not a safety issue.

In our attempt to be responsible parents, we sometimes think our job is to protect our children from *all* pain—both kinds. But the first kind of pain is part of living and growing up. The second kind of pain, however—the type that produces damage—is what we're striving to protect our children from. Understanding the difference is not easy.

chaos \ 'kay oss \ noun:
> A place or circumstance of confusion or disorder.
> A place or setting where safety is compromised.

With these definitions behind us, let's look at the first rule recorded in human history. God said, "Do not eat." Why? Because "if you eat, you will die." That's definitely a safety issue. It's all about damage (see Genesis 2:17).

Rules aren't for modifying behavior, instilling values, or changing attitudes. Here's where parents often go astray, creating regulations that attempt to do exactly those things.

It doesn't work. If you want to see behavioral change, instill values, or work on attitudes, you will model, mentor, teach, and pray repeatedly. Just remember, nothing will *make* your preschooler change.

As we explore rule making, let's review the Three Rules of Life:

Rule One: Your preschooler will live and die by his or her own choices. You can't control him or her—even with legitimate rules.

Rule Two: Your preschooler has the right to choose stupid or smart. That's true even though you've instituted all sorts of good rules.

Rule Three: It's your job to make your preschooler's life a little miserable when he or she chooses stupid. When the rules are broken, then dishing out consequences comes into play.

One of the roads between my house and my office is Academy Boulevard. Every day I drive past a sign that states, "Speed Limit 45." There's no sign saying, "You *should* go 45." There's no sign saying, "Please, *please*, go 45." The rule—the civil law—is clearly stated and posted: "Speed Limit 45." That's it.

Does that sign *make* me travel at the speed that's posted? No.

Does that flat piece of metal *control* me in any way? No.

Why? Because I live and die by my own choices, not by road signs. I have the right to choose smart (drive at the posted speed) or stupid (exceed the posted limit). The signs don't have any control over me at all.

So why the speed limit sign? To keep safety in—and chaos out.

Someone at the Colorado Springs Department of Transportation decided that forty-five miles per hour was a speed at which traffic could safely travel on that stretch of road. The limit increases the chances of keeping safety in and chaos out.

Rules don't control your preschooler, just as a sign can't control a driver. Rules also have consequences attached to them, though, just like exceeding the speed limit can result in a one-hundred-dollar traffic ticket.

Rules, Advice, and Suggestions: What's the Difference?

Since your job is to *influence* your preschooler—not *control* him or her—you can use other ways to influence besides instituting rules. Knowing how helps keep the pressure of parenting low. Let's look at your different options.

Rule: "Billy, you have to drink all your water. The consequence if you don't is you can't go outside to play."

Advice: "Billy, be sure to drink all your water. You're going to get thirsty soon because it's hot outside today."

Suggestion: "Billy, it's really hot outside today. You might want to finish off your glass of water before you go out to play. You'll get thirsty real soon."

We give advice to *influence* our preschoolers' choices and the way in which they think. We do it because we want them to act and think wisely. Advice is wise counsel. Advice is *influence*—an attempt to sway, persuade, and encourage your child in a particular direction of thinking and/or action.

Advice is not a law that reaps a consequence if broken. If wise advice is ignored, natural consequences may follow. This is Rule Three in action.

Since you've been "around the block" more years than your child has, you have accumulated some wise counsel to share. So why do most parents choose to set down rules rather than give advice? Because advice doesn't have the same "bite" that rules have. Advice seems too weak to have any real impact on a preschooler—especially one full of energy all the time.

Suggestions may seem even weaker—just good ideas for making positive choices. A suggestion reflects a good idea or one way to do something. Suggestions are given in an attempt to assist by sharing that common sense you've gained. They're actually another form of influence.

Say What You Mean

Parents can fall into the trap of making "suggestions" to their preschoolers that aren't really suggestions. They are do-it-this-way commands, disguised to sound "nice." If you're giving a suggestion, make sure it really *is* just a suggestion—one your child is free to take *or leave*—without any consequence if it's left.

Does this interchange between a father and his four-year-old daughter, Kelley, sound familiar?

"Kelley, do you want to go to bed now?"

"No, Daddy, I don't want to. After I finish my picture."

"Kelley, you come here right now. It's time for bed like I told you."

Was Kelley's dad "suggesting" she go to bed now? Did he really want to know if she *wanted* to?

Kelley answered with respect and honesty. She didn't *want* to, at least right now. So what's there to be so upset about? Was this a suggestion, or was it really a do-it-now statement? Don't hide rules or commands in "suggestive" verbiage. Your preschooler is a very concrete thinker and will likely take you literally and miss your hint—especially if it's to her benefit!

Here's a better way for Dad to talk to Kelley about bedtime.

"Kelley, it's time to go to bed now." (No *should* or *do you want to*, just a simple, straight statement.)

"I don't want to. After I finish my picture."

"Kelley, I know you want to finish your picture before you go to bed, but it *is* bedtime now. We can put your picture on your nightstand so it will be waiting for you when you wake up tomorrow." (Translation: "Yes, I heard your voice, and it's still time to go to bed.")

"But Daddy, can I please just finish my picture?"

Option 1: "No, Kelley, it really is bedtime now. Let's get you ready for bed. What story do you want Daddy to read to you tonight?" (Dad affirms Kelley was heard; then he redirects attention to the next action in the bedtime routine.)

Option 2: "How much do you have left on your picture?" (Translation: "Yes, I heard your voice. And since *I'm* in charge, *I'll* consider your request, and then *I'll* make the final decision.")

"Just this one last flower, Daddy. See?"

"Finishing that one flower won't take too long. Okay, I decided to give you five more minutes so you can finish one last flower. Then it's off to bed without any complaints. Got it?"

"Got it."

Knowing the differences between hard-and-fast rules, wise advice, and simple suggestions is important. It's a simple yet effective way to keep undue pressure off your shoulders as well.

Rules Are in the Center of the Target

One of my hobbies is target shooting. I don't hunt. I just like the challenge of trying to put a hole in a piece of paper that's far away. So targets make a lot of sense to me.

We looked at a bull's-eye target in chapter 5 to illustrate the relationship between direct commands, specific principles, and general guidelines. Recalling your mental picture of a target, what ring has the biggest area?

The target's center ring holds the *smallest* area in square inches. That's why it's so hard to hit. Each consecutive ring gets bigger in diameter, taking up more square inches as each gets farther from the center.

Rules are in the center ring of our target illustration. Since rules take up the smallest area, there should be very few *rules*. The ring surrounding the center contains *advice*, so you have more space for giving advice. And the biggest area is reserved for your *suggestions*.

Make sure you and your preschooler understand that rules are rules, advice is advice, and suggestions are suggestions.

Often parents aren't clear about which is which. That confusion can cause us to throw everything into the "rule" category when it suits us—when we're trying to control our preschooler's present or future behavior. A child becomes confused if a parent doesn't have the three concepts separated in his or her own mind.

Seven Suggestions for Making Good Rules

1. *Have as few rules as possible.* Why? You will have to keep track of every rule you make. If you can't remember 19,324

rules, don't expect a preschooler—who isn't interested in most of the rules anyway—to keep track of them.

Since consistency is an important ingredient of parenting, you'll have to make sure the rules are enforced each time they're broken. Do you want to spend your life being the house law enforcement officer?

Rules without consequences are meaningless and encourage your child not to believe you. In addition, every time a rule is broken, you'll have to confront your preschooler as you enforce it.

The more rules you make, the more time you'll spend in the law-enforcement side of parenting. Yes, parenting includes enforcing the rules, but that's just a small part of the job. If you spend too much time on enforcement, you'll have less time for other parenting responsibilities. And it adds pressure, pressure, and more pressure.

2. *Make the rule specific and quantitative.* The vaguer the rule, the more room there is for your child to wiggle out of it. Kids can be good at doing just that. Parents often like rules to be vague and general, so they can mold a rule into whatever form is convenient at the moment.

Having specific and quantitative rules keeps *you* in line too. It forces you to be clear and purposeful about your real meanings and desires. It helps you be consistent when you do have to provide a consequence for your child. It also helps keep any manipulative tendencies in check.

3. *Make sure you can enforce the rule.* Unenforced rules are meaningless. Rules that you can't uphold cause you to feel out of control and frustrated.

You might tell your toddler, "You will *never* pick your nose."

That's a specific, clear rule, but is it one you can enforce all the time?

No. Not unless you plan to handcuff yourself to your child twenty-four seven. How are you going to enforce that rule when your son or daughter is at preschool, on a play date, or in your church's child care program?

A rule you *can* enforce is "No picking your nose when you're around me." You can enforce the rules in your house, when your child is in your line of sight.

"But I don't want my child to pick his nose at all, *ever.*"

That's fine. But can you enforce it as a *rule*? No. Besides, is it really a *safety* issue? No.

So you can teach, mentor, pray, and lead by example, *influencing* without embarrassment or shame time and again. A rule about nose picking has to be enforceable—and it's not. *Sigh.*

Relax. He'll get it figured out before he's thirty.

4. *Ask yourself, "Is this a hill worth dying on?"* Is this rule worth all the effort, fight, or confrontation? If it is, because it's actually keeping safety in and chaos out, then fight to win. If it's important—but not worth dying over—relegate it to the advice category. But don't make it a rule. Pick your battles carefully.

5. *Be sure your motive—your reason for this rule—is a good one.* There's a difference between rules, which have consequences attached, and advice about wise behavior and treatment of other people. Violating advice doesn't result in a consequence (because no law has been broken). Of course, disregarding good advice might prompt conversation and teaching as necessary. Keep the goal in mind: to make it

"ouch" a bit when a child chooses stupid, not to control your preschooler or *make sure he or she turns out right.*

6. *Realize that some rules will transform into advice as your child gets older.* That may take some time, so put this suggestion in your pocket and remember it for later.

When our daughters were in their early teens, we had an official rule. When they were going out they needed to get our permission first. Then they needed to tell us where they were going, who they would be with, what they would be doing, and when they would be home. Their return time was either set by their curfew or agreed upon beforehand. As they moved into their later teenage years, this rule was "downsized" to the category of advice. No longer was there a consequence if they didn't provide the information. We did ask these same questions, and if they forgot to provide the information, they were reminded for the future. But no consequence was given.

Why? Because letting us know their plans was a wise practice as well as a courtesy to others in the house. It's on the smart list, and it's a wise practice and show of respect to others. Becky and I would share the same information with our daughters whenever we headed out of the house. Yes, we modeled the behavior we wanted them to practice, but we did so because it was respectful and it was on the smart list.

Moving an issue from a rule to advice allows you to switch from law-enforcement duty to fill your role as a teacher, mentor, reminder, and encourager. That's better than always having to be the "bad guy."

7. *Rules need to be reviewed, updated, and cleaned out periodically.* This is another suggestion for later years, but

it's good to remember it so you can be proactive in your parenting.

Are your rules clear and current? Are there any you can remove from the list to keep things simpler and easier for everyone in the family?

Principles for Instituting Consequences

1. *Make sure you have control over the consequence you plan to give out.* It's vital to make sure you can carry out the consequences attached to any rule. Just as the rule needs to be enforceable by you, the consequence needs to be something you can mete out.

2. *Make sure consequences are specific, limited, and measurable.* Parents often mistakenly dish out a consequence with no clear end to it. Or they attach a phrase such as "You have to earn it back."

Consequences need to be specific and limited. If you choose to give your son a time-out, make sure the "time in" has a distinct "time end" to it. If you take the finger paints away from your daughter, make sure she knows when she'll get them back.

The reason for this is simple. Consequences exist to make it "ouch" a bit after a stupid choice. When you say, "You need to earn it back" or "When you're responsible enough—" or "When we see enough of your behavior change, then—" you're trying to control her behavior rather than provide a true consequence.

This is especially important when working with a preschooler who is not only a very concrete thinker but has no real sense—yet—of time. Besides, three days feels like half a lifetime to a three-year-old. How many things do you remember from half your lifetime ago?

Remember, rules are to keep safety in and chaos out. Consequences are to make life a little bit miserable when a rule has been broken. Even with good rules and good consequences, there are no guarantees.

3. *Keep the consequence connected to the broken rule as much as is practically possible.* If your daughter grabs a doll away from her friend, then your daughter will lose the privilege of playing with that doll for the remainder of the day or play date.

If your toddler throws his Cheerios on the floor, he helps you clean them up. He probably won't be a great help, but he can hold the trash can or do another simple task that includes him in the cleanup process.

These are just a few examples. Be creative when you connect the consequence to the behavior that broke the rule.

Be smart and purposeful when making rules. Learn to separate rules, advice, and suggestions properly.

Giving Grace—Or Is It Mercy?

With all this talk about rules and consequences, where does grace fit in? As Christians, aren't we supposed to extend grace toward our children?

In addressing that question, let me offer a common definition for grace and mercy:

Grace: GETTING something I do NOT deserve.

Mercy: NOT getting something I DO deserve.

When talking about consequences (which your preschooler deserves when he or she breaks a household rule), we're really talking about *mercy* rather than *grace*.

Mercy and consequences—and rules for that matter—aren't mutually exclusive. Here's a suggestion from one parent to another: I extend mercy when I see my daughter's "I got it" expression because that means she learned from her poor choice, which is the ultimate goal. I extend mercy when I understand that applying the legitimate consequence—which she seems willing to accept—wouldn't help her "get it" any more than she just "got it."

Under those circumstances, I'm willing to NOT give her the consequence she DID deserve. I'm more than willing to extend mercy to my daughter because the lesson *was learned*. Mission accomplished.

As you may expect, preschoolers need repetition and reinforcement before the lesson really gets "gotten." During these early years, there will be lots of love and consequences but little mercy—until your child truly begins to "get it" for real.

Homework Assignment

If you could have only five household or family rules, which five would you choose? Remember, these rules are aimed at keeping safety in and chaos out, and *all* family members are included. Write a list of your five rules. Be sure they are specific, clear, and enforceable. Cover everything you deem important for safety, but limit your list to five. By the way, no rule may have sixty-five sub-rules!

I gave this assignment to Gary and Rita as I helped them

work with their three-year-old son, Jared. Rita came back a week later with nine pages of rules. Her typewritten, single-spaced pages consisted of only five numbered rules (per my assignment), but each rule had multiple sub-rules. Rita was trying to pack as much as she could into those five rules. Her real motive was to control Jared's every behavior and attitude.

I sent the couple home to redo the assignment and create five simple, clear rules. By the next appointment, Rita had pared her nine pages down to "only" three pages—still typewritten, still single-spaced. "It was the best I could do," she pleaded. Still, she had too many attachments to each of the five original rules. We talked about the reason for rules and Rita's reasons for her three pages of rules. Again, I sent Rita and Gary home with the same assignment.

Do you see what Rita was trying to do? She was trying to compress every part of life into the target's bull's-eye with line after line of *should* commands.

Was it working for her?

No. By the end of their third session, they understood the assignment and wrestled through their personal motives for trying to control Jared. They also understood they couldn't control him; it wasn't their job. They were still able to make and enforce rules as they saw fit—to keep safety in and chaos out.

What will your five *rules* be? Define the areas that fall under advice or principles you choose to teach. Also, make a list of the important items that fall under the category of suggestions.

There's nothing magical or psychological about the number five. The purpose of this assignment is to help you think simply, clearly, and specifically. If you end up with a *few* more than five rules, it's fine. But think small. I hope your rules will be clear in your own mind, so you can clearly state them to your preschooler.

Focus on the things you *can* control and influence rather than the things you *can't*. Write rules using the HOLD style of interacting. Focus on blending "what I *can* control" with "what I take responsibility for."

Rules written using the GRAB style of interacting mix "what I *can't* control" with "what I take responsibility for." Avoid these. They are doomed to fail.

Remember, household rules are for everyone in the family to follow.

The Issue of Respect

One or more of your house rules may involve behaviors that deal with disrespect toward you and/or others in the house. It's important to have the issue of respect addressed in house rules because disrespect can be a safety issue—physical, emotional, and/or mental safety. Disrespect can easily cause chaos as well. It's appropriate to address the subject of disrespectful behavior when talking about rules of the home.

The most common definition of *disrespect* is *anything you're doing that I don't want you to be doing right now*. This is *not* a good definition. Here are some typical examples:

- Andrew says five-year-old Jeremy is being disrespectful because he's disagreeing with Daddy's decision, when all Jeremy was trying to do was verbalize his frustration.

- Vanessa says it's disrespectful when her four-year-old daughter rolls her eyes and shakes her head.
- Chris, a father of four children under age five, feels strongly that *any* show of anger is disrespectful, regardless of how the kids express it.
- Margarete, a single mom, asks her son if he wants to go to bed now. When he replies, "No, how about later?" she feels disrespected because her "request" isn't met with immediate obedience.

Do any of these situations sound familiar to you? Gaining a healthy and accurate understanding of respect and disrespect will help you in any family dynamic.

Take out a piece of paper and write a clear, simple definition of *disrespect*. Don't consult a dictionary just yet. Write your personal definition first. After you've polished it, compare your definition with a dictionary's. How closely does your definition match it?

Question: Is disrespect an action or an attitude?

Answer: It's both.

Rules are designed to keep safety in and chaos out, so rules are meant to address the unsafe *behaviors* inherent in disrespect. Advice, teaching, and mentoring address the *attitude* aspect of disrespect. You need both. Just be sure to keep them separate.

It's so important to grasp the learning process of children that I'm repeating this principle: Your preschooler is a concrete thinker, so he or she doesn't understand abstract, "deeper thinking" concepts. It's safe to say your toddler doesn't understand the concept of disrespect—the *attitude* part—just yet.

He or she can, however, understand unacceptable *behaviors* because behaviors are concrete. When it comes to respect and disrespect, focus your rule(s) on behaviors, and use advice and suggestions to address the attitude.

Here's a starter list to help you develop a specific definition of *disrespect*. Disrespect is:

- physical violence, or threats of physical violence
- physical posturing—bullying, etc.
- destruction of property, or threats of destruction
- verbal cursing at someone
- verbal name-calling
- verbal condemnations—"I hate you!" etc.

With this list as a start, clarify your household definition of disrespect. Remember, the rule(s) will focus on the specific, unacceptable, unsafe *behaviors*. Unwanted or unacceptable *attitudes* will be addressed with teaching, mentoring, and so forth.

Use this chapter as a guide to help you make and clarify effective rules for your home. One more thing: The house rules are for *everyone* in the house to follow, not just the children. Some rules may be age specific. That's normal. But parents must follow the rules as well. This is especially true when it comes to any rule about being disrespectful toward others in the house. It's hard to enforce rules that you refuse to follow.

Are rules necessary?

Yes, they keep us safe and out of chaos.

Is advice important?

Again, yes. Giving advice is essential to the learning process.

Are suggestions valuable at all?

A hundred times so. They teach and give your preschooler a voice at the same time.

But these aren't nearly as important as *validating* and *nurturing* your preschooler. Rules, advice, and suggestions can smother the validation and nurturing you give. Rules, advice, and suggestions can also be foundational in validating and nurturing your preschooler. Rules and consequences are necessary, but they play second fiddle to *validate* and *nurture*.

Lead by example first. Enforce rules second. "Actions speak louder than words" is a good rule of thumb when it comes to the issue of respect.

TEN

MORE PEACE, LESS STRESS

When dealing with parent/child dynamics, it usually isn't long before the issue of anger crops up, whether it's a two-year-old's tantrum or the frustration of the parent who's dealing with the two-year-old throwing the tantrum.

The word *anger* represents a broad continuum of emotions ranging from a feeling of annoyance (mild) to pure, out-of-control rage (wild). The milder forms of anger are perhaps acceptable and less threatening, but the wilder forms are often too scary for us to deal with effectively, so we shut down all forms of anger—or attempt to shut them down. Anger, frustration, upset, and any number of colorful phrases describe this sensation so common in our daily lives, and we need to address the subject openly and honestly.

"But what's anger got to do with lowering the pressure

when parenting my preschooler?" you might ask. "When somebody's angry, doesn't that mean that person did what they *shouldn't* have done—or is doing something they *shouldn't* be doing?"

Not necessarily.

That's the reason for this chapter. I'm addressing this material to you as a parent—whether or not you ever get angry, frustrated, or annoyed. You can use this information as a template for talking with your preschooler. That way we can get two birds with one stone. Here we go.

Righteous Anger

Righteous anger is a healthy, normal response to an injustice being committed. If you see another parent slap his or her child in the face, I hope the emotion of righteous anger wells up inside you. It's wrong to slap a child in the face.

But even with righteous anger, you're still responsible for how you express it. Here again comes the smart list and stupid list. Choose purposefully and wisely.

Psychological Anger

Anger is a secondary emotion, which means it comes into existence when two other emotions collide. While anger is just another emotion—neither bad nor good—it can be misused or misinterpreted easily. It can also have a very destructive side. Maybe that's why we tend to fear it.

The simple formula for anger is as follows:

$$HURT + WORRY = ANGER$$

Whenever you mix vinegar and baking soda, you get bubbles. Whenever you mix hurt (in the form of disappointment, pain, loss of some kind) and worry, you get anger, frustration, rage, or that sense of annoyance.

That's the formula, and it works the same for parents as it does for preschoolers. Whenever a person is angry, then hurt or disappointment is present as well as worry. And when anger is expressed in actions, it often focuses on trying to force an outcome or control a person or circumstance. Maybe the formula seems a bit simple, but it's a good place to start when trying to understand this emotion. Besides, your toddler's or preschooler's thinking and reasoning is simple, so a simple formula works well. Let's look at each component separately.

The Hurt Feelings

Hurt is that sense of sadness, disappointment, pain, or what we call the "bummer" part of life. Don't go looking into your long-forgotten past for some deep psychological "unfinished business" stemming from your childhood. Hurt is a reaction to an event *in the present moment* that hurts physically, emotionally, or relationally. This hurt may remind you of similar feelings from the past, but it is always a present-tense hurt. Your four-year-old doesn't have much of a "long-forgotten" past anyway, so when they feel hurt, it's caused by something happening in the present.

Ask yourself, what are you disappointed about? What part of life isn't going the way you were expecting or wanting? What hope or dream is being shattered? What damage just occurred? These questions will help you understand the hurt component.

Do you know how to effectively deal with disappointment and sadness? The solution isn't to ignore it or give in to it. What do you do with pain and sadness that life throws your way? Have you learned healthy ways to handle it? What works for you may be worth teaching to your preschooler because it may just work for him or her, too.

Of course, different personalities react in their own ways, and that's why it's important to know what works for you. This understanding will help you notice the signals your preschooler is sending you when he or she is angry.

When we parents are feeling pain from our preschooler's choices, we want to make the pain stop for ourselves and for our child. So we tend to step in and "fix" or overcontrol the situation (GRAB).

When tempted to GRAB, remember to use the two healthy styles of interacting: HOLD (when it's yours to own and be responsible for) and FOLD (when it's your child's to own and take the responsibility for). This is true even when we're dealing with hurt.

The Worry Feelings

Of the three emotions—hurt (sadness), worry, and anger—which one is the most dangerous?

If you guessed anger, you're in the majority.

But you're not correct.

"Yes, but *what if* my child throws one of his first-class fits while we're in the grocery store? *That's* dangerous, let me tell you."

But you're not in the store and he's not throwing a fit *right now.*

"Oh, but he will. It's just a matter of time before it will happen, I'm sure of that. And *what if* it happens—"

Slow down and step out of Stress Trap Two. Stay in the present with me and with the book in your hands.

The sample conversation above demonstrates my point: Worry is the most dangerous emotion because it takes control away from you, causing you to feel or act out of control, even when nothing bad is happening. The nonexistent future has no limits, boundaries, borders, so *anything* is possible. Reality is limited to what is present and real. And it's a much smaller part of the universe to manage. It keeps your stress level down too.

If we can stay away from Stress Trap Two, a whole lot of pressure is removed. And when we take the worry out of the formula, it looks like this:

HURT + (nothing here) = not ANGER

You won't get as angry with worry removed from the formula. But even if anger is absent, you'll still have the hurt. *Sigh.*

When you feel angry, realize a *what-if* statement or two is lurking in your thinking, whether or not you're aware of it. When your preschooler is feeling angry, there's a *what-if* lurking in his or her thinking too. But your young child is likely clueless about the *what-if.* That's where you come in. Do your best to show and verbalize what worries your child. You can still address the worry to soothe and calm her, even if she can't fully comprehend it yet.

Consider the example of three-year-old Micah throwing a fit when it's nap time. (I'm sure this never happened in your house, but maybe the example will benefit the *other* parents reading this book.) Mom says it's time for the afternoon nap, and Micah blows up in a tantrum.

What's the hurt here for Micah? (Don't get overly psychological on me now.)

Micah has to stop playing, so he feels sadness. He loves to play, and he's disappointed because he has to stop doing something he loves. That's pain down to his soul (or so he thinks).

"No, Mommy!" he shouts as frustration overwhelms him.

So what's the worry for a rambunctious three-year-old boy?

Think like a three-year-old here. Taking a one-hour nap in the middle of the day seems to him like he's sleeping half his life away. Without being fully aware of it, he begins worrying: "*What if* I miss out on something?" "*What if* something really cool happens and I don't get to be a part of it?" "*What if* my toys disappear while I'm asleep?" "*What if* Mommy leaves me?"

So when the hurt mixes with the worry, Micah goes *kaboom* and here comes the tantrum.

The same formula fits if you're a six-foot-eight professional football player and you get pulled from your linebacker position after a missed tackle. The same formula fits if you're the parent of a screaming little guy named Micah.

Hurt and worry are always lurking somewhere.

What's the hurt for a grown athlete? Think about what it's like getting pulled from the game. Is it enjoyable to sit on the bench watching another player in your position? There's the disappointment. You aren't playing the game you love. Bummer! That's as complicated as this part gets. No, you wouldn't end up in a hospital psychiatric ward because of this, but it's still a disappointment.

When there's anger, there's worry. Think about all the linebacker's possible *what-if* questions as he sits on the sidelines:

- "*What if* coach doesn't put me back in the game?"
- "*What if* my sub outplays me and I lose my starting position?"
- "*What if* I lose my chance for commercial endorsements because of this?"

Like hurt, worry is not pleasant. Humans naturally want to get away from unpleasant stimuli. Here, again, is where parents are lured into the GRAB style of interacting. In an attempt to get out of Stress Trap Two and avoid the catastrophic outcome our own *what-if* thinking has conjured up, we're tempted to step in and GRAB ownership of what's not ours to control. The pain and disappointment may stem from your preschooler's stupid choices. The worry, though, stems from your *own* unhealthy *what-if* thinking pattern.

Even though you hurt for her and care, don't GRAB; HOLD or FOLD. Don't let anger trick you into GRABing for control. HOLD on to your own anger, deal with it, and then decide what action you need to take with your preschooler.

Remember the principles from chapter 4 when working through worry thinking, and be aware of the subtle way it can contribute to your child's anger or the anger you may feel when confronted with power struggles, rebellion, and misbehavior.

The Angry Feelings

The feeling of anger is usually clearly identifiable at this age. It's known universally as the two-year-old tantrum episode. Its underlying disappointment or hurt may be somewhat easy to identify. The worry behind the anger, however, could take some real searching to find. Your young child may not be ready to put his or her worries into words, but that's not an issue really. Do your best to address your child's worries with your actions and words anyway. If you can't identify his or her worries, take your best guess, and *validate* and *nurture* as you try to calm your child. Bring him or her out of FUTURE thinking and back into the real, PRESENT world. Comfort with words such as these:

- "Honey, can you feel my arms hugging you tightly?"
- "Here, take a sip of water."
- "Open up your fist and squeeze my hand."

Ask questions and suggest simple actions that are physical and tangible, requiring your child to focus on the here and now.

What to Do with Anger

"So what can I do when I'm already angry? What do I do with that emotion?"

Great question. There are two rules for what *not* to do when you are already angry. I'm not a rule-crazy guy, but I can keep track of two rules. By the way, these rules are for you, your preschooler, and everybody else in your family. And they're not that hard to teach, either. Here they are:

Rule One: Don't hurt *others* when angry. Don't hit, attack, bite, spit on, or threaten to hurt another person. Don't hurt with words—by yelling or name-calling. Don't damage others' property (turning Mom's china plates into flying Frisbees, for instance).

Rule Two: Don't hurt *yourself* when angry. Don't bite yourself, slam your fist into the wall, or overdo your working out with weights. Don't hurt yourself with words by calling yourself names or "beating up" on yourself verbally. (Stay out of Stress Trap One.) Don't damage your own stuff by tearing up your favorite pictures or throwing your iPhone across the room.

Here's where doing your homework from the last chapter comes in handy. When you're angry, you're still not to be disrespectful toward others or yourself. Did you make the connection? When you break either of these two rules, you get into trouble. Or maybe a better way to say it is: When you—as a parent—break either of these rules, you create trouble (chaos). That's not good.

Being angry isn't wrong. Expressing anger isn't wrong. It's *how* anger is expressed that can be right or wrong, smart or stupid.

Boy, that sounds familiar, doesn't it?

Here's how to choose smart when the issue of expressing anger comes up:

- Don't hurt others.
- Don't hurt yourself.

With these two rules, I'm encouraging you to choose a smart way to express and deal with your anger in order to avoid the "ouch" that will come if you choose a stupid way of expressing it.

Can you see how these principles are woven together and work in concert with each other?

What *can* you do to express your anger without breaking either rule?

A father came to see me because of his anger issues. After I presented the two rules, he responded, "There's nothing left for me to do!"

Not true. Here's where your creativity can come to life. I've heard many ideas that have worked for people. The sky is the limit. Think it over for yourself. While you're thinking, consider some techniques other parents have tried over the years:

- Amy would go into her bedroom, bury her face in the pillow, and scream. Screaming into the pillow doesn't hurt anybody else's ears (Rule One), and it doesn't hurt her own ears either (Rule Two). She called it a "mommy time-out."

- Julie, another mom I worked with, developed a special code sign she would use with her husband. Julie was able to keep herself together for most of the day. However, if she needed to vent, when her husband returned from work she would give him the code sign. That way, he knew to take over the house for a while. Julie would get into her car and drive on the freeway while screaming at the top of her lungs. Passing drivers thought she was singing to the radio, so it didn't hurt others. When she got her anger out, she turned around, played some mellow music, had a calm drive home, and reengaged with her family.

- Several parents said journaling helps them. The hard thing about journaling is finding the time to journal. If it works for you, fine. If not, don't bother.

- Other parents do something physical: lift weights, go for a walk or run, or clean the house, garage, or kitchen.

- Counting to ten actually does work for some parents.

- Squeezing one of those stress balls can also work. Can't always get to your stress ball in time? Solution: Get *several* stress balls and place them strategically throughout your house. At least one will be close by.

Any number of possibilities may work for you. The important thing is working out a plan and choosing your response in advance, before you actually get angry. That way you won't have to invent a positive action right then and there.

What might be effective for your preschooler? What can you teach him or her to do? Here are several suggestions I've offered to parents over the years. Maybe something here will work or spark an idea for your own child:

- Have your toddler jump up and down until all the "mad" gets shaken out of him. You may need to do it with him, so be prepared to do so.

- Invest in a package of paper lunch sacks. When your preschooler is angry, pull out a bag, open it up, and place it on the floor in the middle of a room. Have your child kick it as hard and as often as he or she wants. Stomping is also allowed. Kicking is a physical activity that helps get the adrenaline out of your child's system. Paper bags make a great noise when kicked, and that "sound of destruction" helps when expending the energy behind anger.

- A favorite idea is teaching your preschooler to growl like a bear when he or she's angry or frustrated. Demonstrate this for your child: Make an angry, scrunched-up face. Then grit your teeth and clench your jaw. Tighten your fists and growl, "Grrrr!" Make your growl long, low, and gruff. I'm still amazed at how often this works for kinesthetic boys. It's physical, no words are required, yet it has great sound effects and engages your child's entire body.

Were you expecting your preschooler to calmly tell you: "Mother, I'm feeling rather angry right now. May we have a spot of tea and talk about it?" Don't hold your breath. Most times for younger children, enlisting physical movement works best.

My older daughter used to get frustrated when something she was trying to do didn't work out the way she wanted. She would yell. In a moment of sheer genius, Becky said, "Terryll, just say 'I'm frustrated' instead of yelling."

A few days later we were both taken by surprise to hear this little voice from the back car seat: "I fuss-tay-tid, Mommy. I fuss-tay-tid!" For some reason known only to God, our two-year-old caught on to the word *frustrated* and began using it.

It's a great word, even for adults. Try it! Say "I'm frustrated," and put some really good tone and energy into it.

You may be surprised what works for you and your child. So go ahead and experiment. Find out what really does help you—and your preschooler, too.

Anger is not an emotion to avoid. Remember that your young child has no clue about how to express his or her anger in a healthy, effective way. You are to teach with your words and your actions. Show your child how a healthy person can and does deal with the emotion of anger when it arises.

ELEVEN

THAT'S A RELIEF:
BRINGING IT ALL TOGETHER

THERE YOU GO. That's low-pressure parenting for preschoolers. *Validate* and *nurture*—and then do it some more.

Okay, it's time for the final exam. Let's see how well the principles of parenting have stuck in your mind. If you can't remember, relax. The answers are at the end of the test. Here we go.

1. What is a dad's primary job in raising a preschooler?
   A. Pay for everything
   B. Be in control of everything
   C. Validate
   D. All of the above

2. What is a mom's primary job in raising a preschooler?

A. Nurture

B. Be in control of everything

C. Keep the house clean and tidy

D. All of the above

3. **If you're a single parent, what do you need to do when raising your preschooler?**

A. Keep your sanity

B. Validate and nurture

C. Do what you can—not what you can't

D. All of the above

4. **What's *not* your job as a parent?**

A. Make sure they turn out right

B. Make sure they turn out right

C. Make sure they turn out right

D. All of the above

5. **What's *not* your other job as a parent?**

A. Make sure you do everything right (perfectly)

B. Make sure you do everything right (perfectly)

C. Make sure you do everything right (perfectly)

D. All of the above

6. **How much validation and nurturing will your preschooler need?**

A. More than I have to give

B. All I have to give

C. Until my child stops whining

D. Enough

7. Which of the following "rules" is *not* part of the Three Rules of Life?

    A. You live and die by your own choices.

    B. You can choose "smart" or choose "stupid."

    C. It's okay as long as you aren't caught.

    D. Somebody or something will make your life miserable when you choose "stupid."

8. What's the key phrase for perfectionistic thinking (Stress Trap One)?

    A. "That's the right way to do something!"

    B. "If you want something done right, you've got to do it yourself."

    C. "If you aren't going to do your best, then don't do it at all."

    D. "I should . . ." or "You shouldn't . . ."

9. What's the key phrase for anxiety (worry) thinking (Stress Trap Two)?

    A. "Oh, my gosh!"

    B. "I don't know . . ."

    C. "What if . . ."

    D. "The sky is falling, the sky is falling . . ."

10. Anger is a mixture of _____ and _____.

    A. Hurt and disappointment

    B. Chips and salsa

    C. Hurt and worry

    D. Boredom and frustration

11. Which word means *to have direct and complete power over?*
    A. Responsible
    B. Liable
    C. Control
    D. Influence

12. Which word means *to take ownership of, to be able to respond to?*
    A. Responsible
    B. Liable
    C. Control
    D. Influence

13. Which word means *to affect, impress, bias, sway, or inspire?*
    A. Responsible
    B. Liable
    C. Control
    D. Influence

14. In the following dance, identify which style of relating the parent and the preschooler are using.

    PARENT: "Oh, honey, you know we don't mark on the table."

    CHILD: "But *you* made me!"

    PARENT: "No, I didn't make you. You did that yourself."

    CHILD: "Yes, you did. *You* didn't give me enough paper to finish my drawing."

    PARENT: "You could have asked for more paper.

That was your choice, and it was a foolish choice to mark on the table."

CHILD: "But . . . *you* . . ."

PARENT: "Enough arguing. Let's get the cleaner and get the marks off the table. You will lose the use of your crayons for the rest of the day because you made a foolish choice."

    A. Parent = HOLD and Child = FOLD

    B. Parent = TOSS and Child = GRAB

    C. Parent = FOLD and Child = TOSS

    D. Parent = GRAB and Child = HOLD

15. **In the following dance, identify which style of relating the parent and the preschooler are using.**

PARENT: "Oh, honey, you know we don't mark on the table."

CHILD: "I sorry, Mommy. I sorry."

PARENT: "Don't worry. I should have given you more paper so you wouldn't run out. Here's more paper. Finish your drawings while I clean off the marks on the table."

CHILD: "I sorry, Mommy. I sorry."

PARENT: "Enough now. Back to your drawings."

    A. Parent = HOLD and Child = FOLD

    B. Parent = TOSS and Child = GRAB

    C. Parent = FOLD and Child = TOSS

    D. Parent = GRAB and Child = HOLD

16. **Which *two* of the following statements describe the reasons for making rules?**

    A. To keep your blood pressure down

B. To keep safety in

C. To keep chaos out

D. To change your preschooler's attitude

17. Which of the following statements are *not* principles to consider when deciding on a consequence for a broken rule?

A. Make sure it will guarantee they never do it again.

B. You need to be able to enforce the consequence you mete out.

C. Consequences need to be clear and limited in length.

D. Tie an "attitude change" clause to getting the privilege back.

ANSWERS

1. C. Validate
2. A. Nurture
3. D. All of the above
4. D. All of the above
5. D. All of the above
6. D. Enough
7. C. It's okay as long as you aren't caught.
8. D. "I should . . ." or "You shouldn't . . ."
9. C. "What if . . ."
10. C. Hurt and worry
11. C. Control
12. A. Responsible
13. D. Influence
14. C. Parent = FOLD and Child = TOSS
15. D. Parent = GRAB and Child = HOLD
16. B. To keep safety in; C. To keep chaos out
17. A. Make sure it will guarantee they never do it again; D. Tie an "attitude change" clause to getting the privilege back.

Repetition is good for preschoolers.

Repetition is good for parents of preschoolers.

Repetition is good for preschoolers and parents.

A Doable Job

You can't make them turn out right. That's *not* your job or your fault.

You won't do everything exactly right (perfectly). That's okay; it's *not* your job either.

You *can* validate and you *can* nurture—whether there are two parents in the home or you're parenting solo. These are the most important, above-all-else items on your job description—*validate* and *nurture*.

You *can* live by—and teach—the Three Rules of Life. That's doable too. You *can* give your preschooler a voice, and you *can* acknowledge your child's God-given free will. You *can* teach your child about the smart list and stupid list.

In our make-sure-they-turn-out-right-and-do-everything-right-control-freak society, we come face-to-face with the age-old spiritual struggle of surrender. I don't hear surrender preached much nowadays, but it's still a critical part of our spiritual maturity. If I asked you on Sunday, "Who's in charge of looking out for your child—you or God?" you'd most likely answer, "God." What you might not say aloud, though, is *as long as He keeps my child safe the way I want Him to.*

Just a few days before writing this chapter, I had a conversation much like this with Sarah regarding her two-and-a-half-year-old son. Sarah is a single parent with joint custody of Luke. When Luke was at his father's apartment, he came across some pornography his father had. When Luke returned to Sarah, he asked why some mommies (to Luke, all adult females were mommies) don't wear any clothes. She was devastated, and rightly so. The court orders, however, mandated joint custody, so Sarah was stuck following those orders in spite of the unhealthy way Luke's father parented. This is a hard, painful reality of FOLDing: "what I can't control" and "what I don't take responsibility for."

Sarah wants to be responsible for Luke's safety—physical and emotional—all the time. Because then she can make his life turn out the way she wants it to—or so her illusion goes. She wants God to be the One who looks out for Luke—as long as God does it according to her specifications. In Sarah's theology, God is sovereign, and that's fine with her (as if God needs her permission to be sovereign). But in her everyday living, she wants that position of absolute control—at least when it comes to Luke.

Sarah called me because her illusion of control and her illusion that her prayers could "make" God do what she wanted Him to do (keeping Luke safe according to her specifications) had been shattered. Sarah wanted her illusions back. She wanted a feeling of control over all situations involving Luke. She wanted to know how things could be like they "used to be" (back in her nice, tidy, illusion-filled way of seeing the world).

As we talked, I gently and caringly pressed Sarah with several questions:

"Who's the one really in charge of Luke—you or God?"

"Is God *really* sovereign all the time, or only when Luke's with you?"

"Was God not aware of this as it happened?"

"If God really is in charge, then why are you trying to tell Him how best to care for Luke? Isn't that playing God—in effect making God your 'genie in a bottle' and telling Him how to run Luke's world?"

Sarah followed my questions, wrestled with her own thinking, and answered, "But Luke is *my* son, and *I* don't want him to get hurt. *I* want to be sure he stays safe (by *my* criteria)."

I validated Sarah's parent heart. Notice, though, the pronouns in Sarah's statements: *my, I, I.*

Sarah's story is not unique at all. But no matter how diligently Sarah tried, or how hard you might try, it's not possible to *make sure your child turns out right* and/or to *make sure you do everything right.*

Que sera, sera.

"I *still* don't like that!"

I still agree with you—it's *still* the truth, though.

Hang In There

God *is* sovereign. Hurts *do* happen. Our God *is* bigger than *any* of the hurts this world throws at us—or our children. If you're in a situation like Sarah's, don't try to GRAB for control you don't have. Don't give up and give in either. From the HOLD position, do what you can, not what you can't. Then move to the FOLD quadrant. Here is where you actively live out that surrendered life and acknowledge God is in control of all the things you aren't. Even though your hands are FOLDed, God's hands aren't.

Parenting preschoolers can be scary. It can also be fun, freeing, and without all that pressure on your shoulders.

Remember to shrink your job description. *Validate* and *nurture* over and over again.

Remember to make friends with your child's God-given free will. Give your child a voice and a choice. Model and teach how to use that voice wisely.

Remember to step away from power struggles. HOLD and FOLD when you interact with your child. It will greatly reduce stress and pressure for everyone.

Remember to reduce the rules. Make as few rules as you can, and focus on keeping safety in and (true) chaos out.

When you practice these four overarching, low-pressure parenting principles, you do the parenting job God wants you to do. And the rest is "gravy."

Be Encouraged

As I was putting these final pages together, I came across the results of a 2007 Associated Press–MTV poll of 1,280 young people I had tucked away in my file on parenting.[1] The survey had to do with whether young people (ages thirteen to twenty-four) are happy and what contributes to their happiness.

Your preschooler isn't in this age category yet, but I hope this study encourages you in the here and now.

When asked the open-ended question "What makes you happy?" the *number one* response was "Spending time with family." It wasn't drugs, money, cars, cell phones, or sex. It was "spending time with family." That's the reward—the outcome—of *validating* and *nurturing*.

The poll found out something else from this age group: Nearly 75 percent said *their relationship with their parents* made them happy.

Did you hear that? Teenagers and collegians said that!

Do you need to pick yourself up off the floor?

Yes, that's really good news! Your child may never tell you that. It may not even feel like it will ever be a reality, but that's what the young people in this survey told the pollsters. This parenting thing *is* doable, and we can keep it low-pressure at the same time.

Validate.

Nurture.

Oh yes, be sure to do the "other stuff" too. Just remember, the other stuff is "gravy" and it plays second fiddle to *validate* and *nurture*.

Hang in there and remember to do what you can—not what you can't.

Get it?

"Got it!"

Great. That's low-pressure parenting.

APPENDIX

THE SMART LIST*

* Collected from ancient writings called the book of Proverbs

How to be smart related to governmental authority
> Obey the civil law.

How to be smart with your words and speech
> Tell the truth. Be honest with whatever you say,
> wherever you say it.
> Speak few words. Be careful with your words.
> Listen. Think it over before you respond.
> Keep confidences.
> Don't brag about yourself.
> Say what you mean, and stick to what you say.
> Speak pleasant, uplifting words whenever you can.

How to be personally smart
> Accept teaching, discipline, and correction—don't think
> you know it all already.

Discern what is accurate, factual, and the truth—and
act on it.

Get wise counsel and direction. Don't rely only on your
own thinking.

Purposefully work at becoming wise with experience
(not just having experiences).

Be humble—not haughty, proud, or arrogant.

Take care of your animals.

Be willing to confess your wrongs and correct them
quickly.

Hate falseness. Don't put up with dishonesty.

Hang around wise, smart people, not fools.

Don't believe everything you hear; check things out.

Keep your cool. Don't be "hot tempered."

Work at being patient.

Take the time to understand people. Don't
automatically trust others.

Seek justice and righteousness. Don't be partial or look
for "fairness."

Keep your passions in check with knowledge.

Don't be under the influence of alcohol, drugs, or any
other substance.

Take time to evaluate your own thinking, actions, and
beliefs.

Pay attention to details.

Restrain your behaviors and appetite. Don't be a
glutton.

Be confident and content with what you have and who
you are. Don't envy others.

Finish your work.

Be aware, see danger, and get away before you get hurt.

Guard your heart very seriously—emotionally and
spiritually.

Keep control of your mind and your thinking.

Deal with your brokenness and pain.

Don't take things personally.

Deal with today. Don't wish it were "like the good old
days."

Deal with today. Don't get caught up in the worry over
tomorrow.

Persevere. Keep going and don't give up.

How to be smart with others

Help your neighbor when you are able.

Don't murder.

Work at keeping peace with others.

Don't rebuke, correct, or advise an arrogant, prideful
person.

Be generous and kind toward other people.

Be cautious going into friendships. Let them develop
slowly over time.

Listen to your parents' advice.

If you're a parent, discipline and correct your kids.

Stay away from foolish people—the people who choose
the "stupid" list.

Be cheerful toward other people whenever you can.

Stay away from bribes. Don't give or receive them.

Overlook offenses whenever it's wise to do so.

Stop a disagreement before it turns into an argument.

Honor your parents. Don't ever cheat them.

Let God "right the wrongs" that happen to you. Don't seek revenge.

Be merciful and kind to the poor; don't exploit them.

Stay away from angry people.

Be modest and quiet when your enemy falls. Don't gloat when it happens.

Don't overstay your welcome.

Be kind to your enemy whenever you can.

Don't be the accomplice of a thief.

Treat your parents honorably and with respect.

Keep your hands on your own stuff. Don't steal.

Be satisfied and comfortable with what you have. Don't covet what your neighbor has.

Treat your wife with honor and respect; cherish her.

Treat your husband with honor and respect; defer to his healthy, wise leadership.

Don't be judgmental toward others.

Extend mercy whenever it's wise to do so.

Be kind and gentle toward children.

Make things right with your neighbor before going to worship God.

Mind your own business. Keep your nose out of other people's affairs.

How to be smart related to sex

Stay away from any and all sex that's not with your spouse.

How to be smart in work and business

Work hard and earn an honest living for yourself. Pay
your own way.

Pay your taxes.

Run an honest business.

Don't cosign for another person.

If you're a boss, pay your employees a deserved wage.

Don't "burn out" trying to get rich—show restraint.

Save money for emergencies and to pass along to your
grandkids.

How to be smart related to God

Acknowledge the one true God and let Him be in
charge of your life.

Love God with all you've got, and let His love soak into
you.

Don't misuse any of God's names.

Live out what you say you believe.

Give God a tithe of your income.

Honor the Sabbath day; keep it separate.

THE STUPID LIST*

* In contrast to the Smart List

How to be stupid related to governmental authority

Only obey civil laws when it suits you.

How to be stupid with your words and speech

Lie, deny, and deceive. Don't tell the truth, or be truthful only when it suits you.

Say whatever you think. Be careless with your words.

Don't waste time listening in any situation. Just give your opinion.

Spread other peoples' secrets to the whole neighborhood.

Brag about yourself often.

Don't worry about what you say. You can always change it later.

Talk harshly and disrespectfully to others.

How to be personally stupid

Think you know it all already. Don't accept teaching, discipline, or correction from anybody else.

Shoot from the hip. Don't bother to discern what is accurate, factual, and true.

Rely only on your own thinking. There's no need for counsel from others.

Go there, do that, get the T-shirt, and move on to the next experience.

Behave in a haughty, proud, and arrogant manner.

Neglect your animals.

Don't ever admit you're wrong. Lie or deny so you can get out of trouble.

Let other people get away with being dishonest.

Hang around foolish people—the ones who choose from the "stupid" list.

Be gullible and believe everything you hear. Don't
bother to check things out first.

Let your anger fly.

Be impatient and short-tempered with people.

Automatically trust other people.

Expect "fairness" from others and the world.

Let your passions run wild.

Get drunk or high.

Don't bother understanding your own thinking, actions,
and beliefs.

Be lazy when it comes to details.

Overeat.

Be jealous.

Leave your work unfinished.

Be clueless.

Wear your heart on your sleeve—emotionally and
spiritually.

Let your mind and thinking go unrestrained.

Ignore or avoid dealing with your brokenness and pain.

Take what people say and do personally.

Wish it were like "the good old days."

Let your mind get caught up in the worry over
tomorrow.

Quit whenever the going gets tough.

How to be stupid with others

Let your neighbor fend for himself.

Take another person's life; commit murder.

Be contentious toward others.

Be stingy and rude toward other people.

Make everybody your friend.

Discount your parents' advice.

If you're a parent, spoil your kids and let them do whatever they want.

Be gruff and rude toward other people.

Accept and give bribes.

Point out every offense you can.

Push a disagreement until it becomes a full-blown argument.

Disrespect your parents. Cheat them too.

Seek revenge.

Exploit the poor. Be rude and mean toward them.

Hang around people who have anger issues.

Gloat when your enemy falls.

Mooch off others.

Always be hateful toward your enemy.

Be willing to be the accomplice of a thief.

Be rude to your parents and treat them with disrespect.

Steal—or "borrow."

Think about wanting what your neighbor has.

Treat your wife condescendingly; control her.

Treat your husband with contempt and belittle him; never follow his lead.

Judge and condemn others.

Never show mercy.

Treat children harshly and rudely.

Ignore the issues between you and your neighbor, then go worship God anyway.

Poke your nose into other people's affairs. Be a
busybody.

How to be stupid related to sex

Have an affair.
Have sex with a prostitute.
Have sex with whomever you want.

How to be stupid in work and business

Work only as hard as you have to. Let other people pay
for your obligations whenever you can.
Cheat on your taxes.
Run your business any way you can to make money.
Cosign a loan for another person.
If you're a boss, pay your employees as little as you can.
Do whatever you can to get rich.
Spend all the money you have while you have it.

How to be stupid related to God

Treat God flippantly, or ignore Him and be in charge
of your own life.
Disrespect God. Reject God's love for you.
Use God's names in vain. Use them as curse words.
Talk one way, then live however you like.
Don't give God a tithe of your income.
Blow off the Sabbath day—it's nothing more than
another day off work.

NOTES

CHAPTER SIX
1. Erik H. Erikson, *Childhood and Society* (New York: W.W. Norton & Company, reissued edition 1993).
2. Ibid.
3. Malcolm Gladwell, *Outliers* (New York: Little, Brown & Company, 2008).

CHAPTER EIGHT
1. Peter Gray, "Declining Student Resilience: A Serious Problem for Colleges," *Psychology Today*, September 22, 2015, https://www.psychologytoday .com/blog/freedom-learn/201509/declining-student-resilience-serious -problem-colleges.

CHAPTER ELEVEN
1. Associated Press, *NBC News*, "Youths' Stuff of Happiness May Surprise Parents," August 20, 2007, http://www.nbcnews.com/id/20322621# .Vr4oR7xddlw.

Meet the rest of the family

**Expert advice on parenting and marriage . . .
spiritual growth . . . powerful personal stories . . .**

Focus on the Family's collection of inspiring, practical resources can help your family grow closer to God—and each other—than ever before. Whichever format you need—video, audio, book, or e-book—we have something for you. Discover how to help your family thrive with books, DVDs, and more at **FocusOnTheFamily.com/resources**.

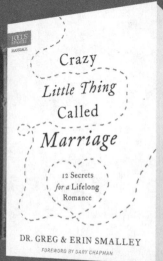
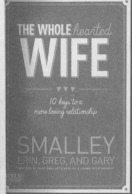